HUME: A GUIDE FOR THE PERPLEXED

THE GUIDES FOR THE PERPLEXED SERIES

HUME: A GUIDE FOR THE PERPLEXED

ANGELA COVENTRY

continuum

Continuum

Continuum International Publishing Group
The Tower Building
11 York Road
London SE1 7NX

80 Maiden Lane
Suite 704
New York NY 10038

www.continuumbooks.com

© Angela Coventry 2007

British Library Cataloguing-in-Publication Data
A catalogue record for this book is available from the British Library.

ISBN-10: HB: 0-8264-8922-2
PB: 0-8264-8923-0
ISBN-13: HB: 978-0-8264-8922-7
PB: 978-0-8264-8923-4

Library of Congress Cataloging-in-Publication Data
A catalog record for this book is available from the Library of Congress.

Typeset by Servis Filmsetting Ltd, Manchester
Printed and bound in Great Britain by MPG Books Ltd,
Bodmin, Cornwall

Dedicated to Martin, Isabella and 'Baby Tummy'

CONTENTS

CONTENTS

ABBREVIATIONS

AB   David Hume, 'An Abstract of a Book lately published entitled *A Treatise of Human Nature* wherein the chief argument of that book is farther illustrated and explained'
taken from THN (see below). References cite the book,
chapter, section, and paragraph to the most recent Oxford
edition followed by page numbers from the Selby-
Bigge/Nidditch editions, prefixed by 'SBN'.

AT   Antoine Arnauld and Pierre Nicole, *Logic or The Art of
Thinking.* Trans. J. V. Buroker, Cambridge: Cambridge
University Press, 1996. References cite page numbers only.

CPR   Immanuel Kant, *Critique of Pure Reason*. Trans. P. Guyer
and A. Wood, Cambridge: Cambridge University Press,
1997. References cite both 'A' and 'B' editions.

CSM   René Descartes, *The Philosophical Writings of Descartes*.
Trans. John Cottingham, Robert Stoothoff, and Dugald
Murdoch, vols. I and II, New York: Cambridge University
Press, 1985, 1993. References cite volume and page
number.

DNR   David Hume, *Dialogues Concerning Natural Religion* (2nd
edn). Ed. Richard H. Popkin, Indianapolis/Cambridge:
Hackett University Press, 1998.

ECHU   John Locke, *An Essay Concerning Human Understanding*.
Ed. P. H. Nidditch, Oxford: Oxford University Press, 1975.
References cite book, chapter and paragraph number.

EHU   David Hume, *An Enquiry Concerning Human
Understanding*. Ed. T. L Beauchamp, Oxford: Oxford
University Press, 1999, and *An Enquiry Concerning
Human Understanding* (3rd edn). Eds L. A. Selby-Bigge

and P. H. Nidditch, Oxford: Clarendon Press, 1975. References cite the book, chapter, section, and paragraph to the most recent Oxford edition followed by page numbers from the Selby-Bigge/Nidditch editions, prefixed by 'SBN'.

EMPL   David Hume, *Essays: Moral, Political, and Literary* (revised edn). Ed. Eugene Miller, Indianapolis: Liberty Fund, 1985. References cite page numbers only.

EPM   David Hume, *An Enquiry Concerning the Principles of Morals*. Ed. T. L Beauchamp, Oxford: Oxford University Press, 1998, and *An Enquiry Concerning Human Understanding and Concerning the Principles of Morals* (3rd edn). Eds. L. A. Selby-Bigge and P. H. Nidditch, Oxford: Clarendon Press, 1975. References cite the book, chapter, section, and paragraph to the most recent Oxford edition followed by page numbers from the Selby-Bigge/Nidditch editions, prefixed by 'SBN'.

HD   Pierre Bayle, *Historical and Critical Dictionary: Selections*. Trans. R. Popkin, Indianapolis/Cambridge: Hackett University Press, 1965. References cite page numbers only.

MP   Isaac Newton, *The Mathematical Principles of Natural Philosophy*. Two vols. Trans. and ed. Andrew Motte and revised by Florian Cajori, University of California, 1962. References cite volume and page number.

OP   Isaac Newton, *Opticks*, Mineola: Dover Publications, 1952. References cite page number only.

PHK   George Berkeley, *A Treatise Concerning the Principles of Human Knowledge*. Ed. K. P. Winkler, Indianapolis: Hackett Publishing Company, 1982. References cite Part and Section number.

PR   Immanuel Kant, *Prolegomena to Any Future Metaphysics That Can Qualify as a Science*. Trans. Paul Carus, Chicago: Open Court Publishing, 1997. References cite page number only.

ST   Nicolas Malebranche, *The Search After Truth*. Eds. Thomas Lennon and Paul Olscamp, Cambridge: Cambridge University Press, 1997. References cite page numbers only.

THN   David Hume, *A Treatise of Human Nature*. Eds. D. F. Norton and M. J. Norton, Oxford: Oxford University

Press, 2000, and *A Treatise of Human Nature* (2nd edn). Eds. L. A. Selby-Bigge and P. H. Nidditch, Oxford: Clarendon Press, 1978. References cite the book, chapter, section, and paragraph to the most recent Oxford edition followed by page numbers from the Selby-Bigge/Nidditch editions, prefixed by 'SBN'.

ACKNOWLEDGEMENTS

Thanks to both Don Garrett and David Owen for their continual support and ongoing inspirational Hume scholarship. Many thanks also to Eric Steinberg for very helpful comments on the penultimate draft of this manuscript. Thanks to all of the students who have taken my various classes on Hume over the years and special extra thanks also to Martin, Isabella and 'Baby Tummy' for the steady supply of distractions, fun and love.

INTRODUCTION

David Hume is arguably the greatest philosopher to have written in the English language. He made significant contributions in epistemology, metaphysics, morality, psychology, politics and social history, economics, history, religion, literary and aesthetic theory. This book attempts an accessible and unified presentation of Hume's most important contributions to epistemology and metaphysics in a manner that does not presuppose any familiarity with Hume on the reader's part. While the present work is written as a guidebook for beginner students, the scholarly debates that surround Hume's philosophy have not been entirely ignored, but I have done my best to keep scholarly detail to a minimum. Further, although this is a work primarily in Hume's metaphysics and epistemology, the topics including the origin and association of ideas, space and time, causal reasoning, necessary connections, free will, personal identity, and scepticism, I have also referred the reader to other areas of work, particularly his views on the passions, morals, aesthetics and religion when appropriate. This work contains, however, no discussion of his politics, history and economic theory.

A final caveat. This work relies more heavily on the structure and detail of *A Treatise of Human Nature*, although material has also been included from *Enquiry Concerning Human Understanding* when judged appropriate. The main reason for this reliance is that the *Treatise* simply, in my eyes, provides a much more complete picture of his philosophy than the much abridged and polished *Enquiry*. Some scholars believe that there are enough substantial differences between the two works to warrant treating them separately. This approach takes seriously Hume's renunciation of the *Treatise* in the Advertisement to the last edition of the *Enquiry*, published 1777, which closes by saying that 'henceforth, the author desires, that the following pieces may alone be regarded as containing his philosophical sentiments and principles'. At the same time however Hume says even in the Advertisement that 'most of the principles, and reasonings, contained in this volume, were published' in the *Treatise*, and that he has 'cast the whole anew in the following pieces, where some negligences in his former reasoning and more in the expression, are . . . corrected'. In his own autobiography also he claimed that the *Treatise*'s lack of success 'proceeded more from the manner than the matter' (EMPL xxxv) and in a letter wrote that 'the philosophical principles are the same in both'.[1] This present work attempts to provide an introduction to Hume's thought that combines the structure and detail of the *Treatise* with much of the clarity and style of the *Enquiry*.

NOTE

1 See Grieg (1932: I, 158).

CHAPTER 1

LIFE AND WORKS OF DAVID HUME

David Hume was born in Edinburgh on 26th April 1711 to Joseph and Katherine Home. Both parents were of a good, although not especially wealthy, background. His father's family is a branch of the Earl of Home's and his ancestors have been proprietors of a modest estate for several generations, while his mother was the daughter of Sir David Falconer, a distinguished lawyer who became President of the College of Justice.[1]

Not much is known about Hume's early childhood and education. It is likely that he spent his childhood divided between the family's Edinburgh house on the south side of the Lawnmarket, the dwelling presumably within which Hume was born, and Ninewells, the family estate on the Whiteadder River in the border lowlands near Berwick. The house at Ninewells stands on a bluff above the waters of the Whiteadder.[2] Down the bluff a few yards to the south-east of the house, an overhanging rock forms a shallow cave where local legend has it he indulged in profound philosophical reflections.[3] Further along the waterside are more caves, quarries and freestone rocks, and it is around these parts where Hume probably played as a young boy with his elder brother John, in addition to engaging in activities like hunting, fishing and horseriding.[4] Since attendance at church was required by law at that time presumably Hume and his family also attended the local Church of Scotland pastored by his uncle.[5]

Just after Hume's second birthday, his father died, leaving him, his elder brother John and sister Katherine under the care of their mother, who 'devoted herself entirely to the rearing and educating of her Children' (EMPL xxxii). His mother reported that her young David was good natured and 'uncommon wake-minded', that is, uncommonly *acute*, in accordance with the local dialect of the period.[6] Indeed his earliest surviving letter from Ninewells dated 4th July 1727, written at the age of sixteen, indicates that he was already engaged in the writing of what would end up being his first and arguably greatest work, *A Treatise of Human Nature: Being an Attempt to Introduce the Experimental Method of Reasoning into Moral Subjects*, the first two volumes of which would be published anonymously by the time he was twenty-seven.[7] Hume himself observes on many occasions that his interest in literature began at a very early age and that most of his life has been devoted to 'literary Pursuits and Occupations'.[8] He claims that since 'earliest Infancy, [he] found alwise a strong Inclination to Books & Literature',[9] that he was 'seized very early with a passion for Literature which has been the ruling Passion of [his] Life, and the great Source of [his] Enjoyments' (EMPL xxxii–xxxiii). However, being the second son of a not very rich family meant that there was not enough money to allow himself full-time devotion to literary pursuits, so he always had to earn a living to supplement his income.

Most likely educated at home by local tutors in addition to his mother's instruction, until at the age of eleven, Hume accompanied his brother to Edinburgh University. His studies there probably included Latin, Greek, logic, metaphysics, moral philosophy, history, mathematics and natural philosophy. He left Edinburgh University in either 1725 or 1726, when he was around fifteen years old, without formally taking a degree to pursue his education privately. His scholarly disposition, coupled with the fact that both his father and maternal grandfather had been lawyers, meant that a career in law was encouraged, but his scholarly interests soon turned to literature and philosophy. In fact, he writes in his autobiography that he 'found an unsurmountable aversion to everything but the pursuits of philosophy and general learning' (EMPL xxxiii). Pursuing the goal of becoming 'a Scholar & Philosopher',[10] he followed a rigorous program of reading, reflection, and taking notes. During this time of private study, he found nothing but 'endless Disputes' even in the most fundamental of matters.[11] Upon this discovery, 'a certain Boldness of Temper' grew within him, leaving him disinclined to trust authorities on any subject. He sought after instead 'some new Medium' by which 'Truth might be establisht'.[12]

In spring 1729 after three years of study, things started to fall into place for the young scholar. He describes how at the age of eighteen, a 'New Scene of Thought' opened up to him, transporting him 'beyond measure'.[13] He applied himself intensely to his studies, until he found himself mentally exhausted. Then after some nine months, physical symptoms emerged with the mental.[14] Scurvy spots appeared on his fingers for which a physician prescribed a product of citrus fruit juices. By April 1730, Hume consulted a physician again to complain of a 'Watryness in the mouth'.[15] The doctor apparently laughed and told him that he had gotten the 'Disease of the Learned', prescribing 'A Course of Bitters & Anti-Hysteric Pills' along with an 'English Pint of Claret Wine every Day' and a long horseback ride.[16] Despite some improvement under the new regime, his condition continued to affect his studies. This time he was unable to comprehend his material as a whole and give it a coherent form; he writes that he was 'not able to follow out any Train of Thought by one continued Stretch of View' but only 'by repeated Interruptions, & by refreshing my eye from Time to Time upon other Objects'.[17] In such a state, there was no chance that he could deliver his work 'with such Elegance & Neatness' so as to draw 'the Attention of the World'.[18]

In 1734, Hume decided to rid himself of his physical and mental condition by entering 'a more active scene of life' (EMPL xxxiii). He went off to Bristol to pursue a business career as a clerk in the office of a West Indies sugar merchant. He quickly found this unsuitable and left for France within a few months determined to pursue his studies. He spent a year in Rheims, and then moved to Le Flèche, a village in Anjou best known for its Jesuit College. Here, where renowned philosophers such as René Descartes (1596–1650) and Marin Mersenne (1588–1648) studied a century before, Hume read French and other continental authors, especially Descartes, Nicolas Malebranche (1638–1715) and Pierre Bayle (1647–1706). He also composed most of his three-volume *A Treatise of Human Nature*. Book I 'Of the Understanding' and Book II 'Of the Passions' were published in the last week of January 1739, and Book III 'Of Morals' was published on 5th November 1740. The *Treatise* explores a variety of philosophical topics such as the origin of ideas, space, time, causality, personal identity, external objects, scepticism, the immateriality of the soul, the passions, free will, and morality. Today it is thought to be his most important work and one of the most important works in the history of philosophy.

He returned to England in mid-September 1737, carrying a manuscript with him. He spent the next year revising the work and arranging for its publication. Hume chose to withhold the section on miracles, some say possibly to avoid giving offence to English theologian and philosopher Joseph Butler (1692–1752), whose endorsement of the work he sought. By September 1738, he signed a contract for the publication of the first two books of the *Treatise* and the books were offered for sale for the price of ten shillings the following January. Early sales of the *Treatise* were disappointing. Hume famously noted that this work '*fell dead-born from the press*, without reaching such distinction, as even to excite a murmur among the zealots' (EMPL xxxiv). He blamed the lack of success of the *Treatise* on stylistic issues, 'proceeding more from the manner than the matter' and admitted of being 'guilty' of publishing the work 'too early' (EMPL xxxv). The *Treatise* was reviewed in various literary journals in both Britain and the Continent, such as the *History of the Works of the Learned* and *Göttingische Zeitungen*.[19] In response to some of the more unfavorable reviews, Hume composed and published an Abstract of the *Treatise* on the 11th March 1740, which was an anonymous sixpenny thirty-two page pamphlet summarizing the main argument in the first book.[20]

After the publication of the first two installments of the *Treatise*, Hume went to live with his mother and brother at his brother's country house and continued to write. In 1741 and 1742, he published *Essays Moral and Political* in two volumes. The *Essays* were published in a series of volumes before being gathered together into one volume near the end of Hume's life. The *Essays* were much better received than the *Treatise* and their success increased his reputation, leading to his candidacy for a philosophy chair at Edinburgh University in the summer of 1744. He withdrew his candidacy, however, due to great opposition by members of the academic community, the Edinburgh clergy and other civic leaders. One or more pamphlet/s even circulated that accused him of advocating extreme scepticism, atheism, and undermining the foundations of morality, to which Hume composed a letter that summarizes and replies to the charges made against him. It was published anonymously as *A Letter from a Gentleman to his Friend in Edinburgh*. In 1751–1752, Hume also sought a Logic chair vacated by his good friend, Scottish philosopher and economist Adam Smith (1723–1790), at the University of Glasgow and was once again unsuccessful because he was deemed a threat to the established religion. Religious opposition remained a recurring theme throughout his life. Hume was nearly excommunicated by the General Assembly of the Kirk, which is the Scottish Church's highest judicial body. In 1756, the case against Hume was brought before a committee of the General Assembly, but a decision was made to drop the matter. In 1761, the Roman Catholic Church put all of his writings on the *Index Librorum Prohibitorum* (*List of Prohibited Books*), the list of forbidden publications censored by the Church.

In 1745, Hume accepted an offer in England to work as a tutor for the young Marquis of Annandale, only to find the Marquis mentally unstable and his estate manager dishonest. That year also his mother died.[21] In 1746, Hume accepted the invitation of a distant relation, Lieutenant-General James St. Clair, to be his secretary on a military expedition against the French in Quebec. The expedition was eventually abandoned, only to take up a new expedition that ended in an unsuccessful raid on the coast of L'Orient in Brittany. Hume also accompanied St. Clair on an extended diplomatic mission to Vienna and Turin in 1748. While he was in Turin, the *Philosophical Essays Concerning Human Understanding* appeared, bearing his name prominently. A recasting of the central ideas of Book I of the *Treatise*, with some added material on miracles and the design argument for the existence of God, the *Philosophical Essays* reached a third edition within three years of its publication, and were eventually reprinted under the title by which they are known today, *An Enquiry Concerning Human Understanding*.

Hume's appointments with the Marquis and St. Clair raised his finances to 'near a thousand pounds' (EMPL xxxv) and in 1749, he returned to his brother's country house for two years. Here, he composed *Political Discourses* (a collection of essays on economic and political subjects) and *An Enquiry Concerning the Principles of Morals* (which recasts Book III of his *Treatise*). In 1751, Hume moved in with his sister in Edinburgh. Soon after his arrival, he was elected joint secretary of the Philosophical Society of Edinburgh, which had been established originally in 1731 to collect and publish essays on medicine and surgery, the scope of which was enlarged to include philosophy and literature in 1737.[22] Under Hume's editorship, two volumes had been published in 1754 and 1756, but he had resigned the post sometime before the third volume was published in 1771. In addition to joining the Philosophical Society in 1751, his *Enquiry Concerning the Principles of Morals* was published that same year. Hume described the second *Enquiry* as 'incomparably the best' of all his works (EMPL xxxvi). The *Political Discourses* appeared in print in 1752, and was an immediate success, reaching a third edition within two years. In 1753, Hume brought together collected editions of his works, excluding the *Treatise* and including *Essays, Moral and Political, Philosophical Essays Concerning Human Understanding, Enquiry Concerning the Principles of Morals*, and *Political Discourses*. The first edition of *Essays and Treatises on Several Subjects* came out in four volumes between 1753–1756 and by 1764 had reached a fourth edition.[23]

On 28th January 1752, Hume received an offer to serve as librarian to the Edinburgh Faculty of Advocates. This opportunity gave him the resources to work on another project, *The History of England*, which was published in six installments between 1754–1762. His *History of England* became a best-seller and was widely regarded as a standard work for many decades, eventually going through over one hundred editions. This work established his literary reputation with eighteeth-century readers. French philosopher Voltaire (1694–1778) even praised his *History* as perhaps the best ever written in any language.

During his stint at the library, Hume also completed writing his two important works in the philosophy of religion: the *Dialogues Concerning Natural Religion* and 'The Natural History of Religion'. The *Dialogues*, a dramatic conversation about religion in twelve parts conducted by three characters, Cleanthes, Demea and Philo, remained unpublished until 1779, some say due to the advice of friends who wished to steer Hume away from religious controversy. The *Dialogues* is widely regarded as not only the greatest work on philosophy of religion in the English language, but also as the best dialogue written in English. 'The Natural History of Religion' was published as part of *Four Dissertations* in January 1757, with 'Of the Passions', 'Of Tragedy' and an essay on aesthetics, 'Of the Standard of Taste'. 'The Natural History of Religion' was originally included in a volume of Hume's essays titled *Five Dissertations*, ready for distribution in 1756 with 'Of the Passions', 'Of Tragedy', 'Of Suicide' and 'Of the Immortality of the Soul'. The latter two essays were removed, some say due to pressure applied by the Reverend William Warburton (1698–1779), who threatened Hume's publisher with prosecution if the essays was published.[24] The printed copies of *Five Dissertations* were altered, without 'Of Suicide' and 'Of the Immortality of the Soul', and with a new, hastily written, essay 'Of the Standard of Taste' inserted in place of the two removed essays. The essays were then bound with the new title *Four Dissertations* and distributed the following year.

His post at the Advocates Library, while extremely productive, was not entirely without controversy. In 1754, he was accused of ordering several 'indecent Books unworthy of a place in a learned Library'[25] and the order was cancelled by the curators. Hume was furious, to say the least, but did not resign because he still needed access to the Library's resources as research for his *History* was not yet complete, although he did donate his salary to a blind poet, Thomas Blacklock. When research for the *History* was done in 1757, Hume promptly resigned.[26]

Around 1761 at the age of fifty, Hume writes that he was 'opulent' by way of money given to him by the booksellers, and he retired to Scotland, 'determined never more to. . .set. . .foot out of it' (EMPL xxxviii). Some two years later, however, Hume left for France again, accepting an invitation from Lord Hertford, the Ambassador to France, to serve as his private secretary. During his three years in Paris, Hume became Secretary to the Embassy and eventually its *chargé d'affaires*. He was very well-received there, indeed, he recorded of the first few weeks in France that he received so much flattery he was confounded and embarrassed, finding that the more he 'recoiled from their excessive Civilities', the more he 'was loaded with them'.[27] He become the rage of the Parisian intellectual salons, enjoying the conversation and company of Denis Diderot (1713–1784), Jean le Ronde D'Alembert (1717–1783), and Baron d'Holbach (1723–1789) and found himself the object of great attention from the ladies at the French court.

Returning to London in 1766, he brought with him Swiss-born philosopher Jean-Jacques Rousseau (1712–1778), who had been ordered out of Switzerland by the government in Berne. Hume offered Rousseau refuge in England, even using his contacts to secure a government pension for Rousseau from King George III. Shortly after arriving in England, however, the friendship dissolved. A rather paranoid Rousseau became suspicious that Hume and some of his friends were plotting against him and that he had been invited to England for the sole purpose of becoming an object of ridicule. Rousseau refused his pension and in a letter to Hume threatened to go public with his accusations. Hume defended himself by preemptively publishing *A Concise and Genuine Account of the*

Dispute between Mr. Hume and Mr. Rousseau, which documents the relevant correspondence between them with a connecting narrative.

After a year (1767–1768) serving as an Under-Secretary of State in London, Hume finally returned to Edinburgh to stay. By autumn of 1770, he was actively supervising in the building of a house on St. Andrew Square in a street which was to become known as St. David's Street.[28] Hume described the process of building a house as the 'second great Operation of human Life'; taking a wife was the first, which he hoped would 'come in time'.[29] He never did marry, however, spending his late years quietly and comfortably, reading, writing and dining with friends in his new house with his sister Katherine and a little pomeranian dog called Foxey. Brother and sister were known for their gracious hospitality. One of their first guests was a visitor from America: Benjamin Franklin (1706–1790). In London soon after Franklin spoke of Hume as one who had 'entertain'd [him] with the greatest Kindness and Hospitality'.[30]

At around 1772, Hume was becoming increasingly ill with a bowel disorder. Three years later, the progress of the decline was rapid. He suffered from high fevers at night, severe diarrhoea and internal haemorrhages. He prepared for his death by going about his usual activities: reading, writing letters, and revising his works for new editions of the *History of England*, and his *Essays and Treatises*, which now contained his collected essays, the two *Enquiries, A Dissertation on the Passions* and 'The Natural History of Religion'. In the Advertisement to the last edition of the *Enquiry*, published in 1777, he calls the *Treatise* a 'juvenile work, which the author never acknowledged' and closes by saying that 'henceforth, the author desires, that the following pieces may alone be regarded as containing his philosophical sentiments and principles'. He also arranged for the posthumous publication of the *Dialogues Concerning Natural Religion*, which was seen through the press by his nephew in 1779. Throughout the period, he remained in good humour and serene spirits. There are accounts of his visits with friends in his final months written by James Boswell (1740–1795), William Cullen (1710–1790) and Smith. Boswell lured him into a conversation about immortality and was then astonished to discover one who faced the prospect of his own imminent death with complete equanimity and good spirits. In his 'An Account of My Last Interview With David Hume, Esq.', Boswell writes that when he met with Hume on 7th July 1776, he 'asked him if it was not possible that there might be a future state'. He answered 'It was possible that a piece of coal put upon the fire would not burn; and he added that it was a most unreasonable fancy that he should exist for ever'.[31] Hume died on Sunday, 25th August 1776 at about four o'clock in the afternoon.

After his death, previously unpublished works appeared. The first was a short autobiography, 'My Own Life', which was published with a letter by Smith written soon after Hume's death. In this letter, he famously writes of Hume: 'upon the whole, I have always considered him, both in his life-time and since his death, as approaching nearly to the idea of a perfectly wise and virtuous man, as perhaps the nature of human frailty will admit'.[32] Two years later, in 1779, Hume's *Dialogues Concerning Natural Religion* appeared. Finally, in 1783, the suppressed essays on suicide and immortality were published. This edition was a reprint of an anonymous copy of the essays circulated in 1777; another anonymous copy had appeared previously in French seven years earlier. Along with Hume's two essays, the editor of the 1783 edition included anonymous critical responses to both pieces with excerpts from Rousseau's *La Nouvelle Heloise* on the subject of suicide.

1.1. PUBLICATION TIME-LINE

1739	*A Treatise of Human Nature: Being an Attempt to Introduce the Experimental Method of Reasoning into Moral Subjects*, Book I 'Of the Understanding' and Book II 'Of the Passions'
1740	(a) *A Treatise of Human Nature*, Book III 'Of Morals' (b) *An Abstract of a Book lately Published; entituled, A Treatise of Human Nature, &c. Wherein the chief Argument of that Book is farther Illustrated and Explained*
1741–1742	*Essays Moral and Political*
1745	*A Letter from a Gentleman to his Friend in Edinburgh: Containing Some Observations on a Specimen of the Principles concerning Religion and Morality, said to be maintain'd in a Book lately publish'd, intituled, A Treatise of Human Nature*
1748	*Philosophical Essays Concerning Human Understanding*, later titled *An Enquiry Concerning Human Understanding*

1751	*An Enquiry Concerning the Principles of Morals*
1752	*Political Discourses*
1753–1756	*Essays and Treatises on Several Subjects*
1754–1762	*The History of England from the Invasion of Julius Cæsar to the Revolution in 1688*
1757	*Four Dissertations*
1766	*A Concise and Genuine Account of the Dispute between Mr. Hume and Mr. Rousseau: with the Letters that Passed between them during their Controversy*
1777	'My Own Life'
1779	*Dialogues Concerning Natural Religion*
1783	'Of Suicide' and 'Of the Immortality of the Soul'

NOTES

1 See the second paragraph of Hume's autobiography 'My Own Life'. References to 'My Own Life' are taken from EMPL with page numbers.
2 See Mossner (1980: 20–21).
3 Mossner (1980: 22).
4 Mossner (1980: 20–22).
5 Mossner (1980: 32–33).
6 Fate Norton: (1993:2). This remark by Hume's mother is recorded in Burton (1846: I, 294n).
7 Mossner (1980: 62–63).
8 Grieg (1932: I, 13).
9 Grieg (1932: I, 13).
10 Grieg (1932: I, 13).
11 Grieg (1932: I, 13).
12 Grieg (1932: I, 13).
13 Grieg (1932: I, 13).
14 Mossner (1980: 66).
15 Mossner (1980: 67).
16 Mossner (1980: 67).
17 Mossner (1980: 70).
18 Mossner (1980: 70).
19 For a thorough discussion of the initial reception of the *Treatise*, see Mossner (1980: Part I, chapter 10), and Mossner (1947: 31–43).
20 The original announcement in *The Daily Advertiser* of March 11th 1740 described the title of the pamphlet as: 'An Abstract of a Late Philosophical Performance, entitled *A Treatise of Human Nature, &c.* Wherein the chief Argument and Design of that Book, which has met with such Opposition, and been represented in so terrifying a Light, is further illustrated and explain'd.'
21 The exact date of her death is unknown but it took place before the middle of June that year at which time Hume wrote in a letter that he

was receiving 'melancholy' letters from his brother, noting that his mother's death 'makes. . .an immense void in our Family', Grieg (1932: I, 17).

22 Mossner (1980: 257).

23 Mossner (1980: 224).

24 Mossner (1980: 324).

25 The offensive books included the *Contes* of Jean de La Fontaine (1621–1695) and Roger de Bussy-Rabutin's (1618–1693) *Historie amoureuse des Gaules*. He wrote that, 'if every book not superior in merit to *La Fontaine* be expelled from the Library, I shall engage to carry away all that remains in my pocket. I know not indeed if any will remain except our fifty pound Bible, which is too bulky for me to carry away. . .By the bye, *Bussy Rabutin* contains no bawdy at all, though if it did, I see not that it would be a whit the worse', see Mossner (1980: 252–3).

26 Mossner (1980: 253).

27 Mossner (1980: 443).

28 Mossner (1980: 562).

29 Mossner (1980: 566).

30 Mossner (1980: 573).

31 Mossner (1980: 597–8).

32 Mossner (1980: 604–5).

CHAPTER 2

INTELLECTUAL HERITAGE

Hume is commonly classified as the last of the three great British empiricists following in the tradition of John Locke (1632–1704) and George Berkeley (1685–1753) in the Early Modern period of philosophy, which spans roughly the seventeenth and eighteenth centuries. The Early Modern period is noted for its remarkably high level of philosophical activity, no doubt linked to significant developments in science, religion and culture.[1] To understand what it means to be classified a British empiricist at this time in the history of philosophy it is prudent to begin with the growth of science.[2]

2.1. THE GROWTH OF SCIENCE

In 1543, astronomer Nicolaus Copernicus (1473–1543) published *Revolutions of Heavenly Spheres*. In this work, which was censored by the Catholic Church, Copernicus produced arguments that the earth revolved around the sun, thereby discovering the heliocentric or sun-centered model of the solar system. Copernicus' heliocentric theory of the universe was entirely mathematical, in the sense that the predictions of the observed positions of celestial bodies were based on an underlying geometry. The heliocentric theory challenged the traditional belief, held by medieval thinkers, that the planets and stars revolved around the earth, which was assumed as the center of the universe. This gave rise to what became known as the 'Copernican Revolution'.

German astronomer Johannes Kepler (or Keppler) (1571–1630) and Italian scientist Galileo Galilei (1564–1642) also made significant contributions to the growth of science. Following Copernicus, Kepler also applied mathematical principles to astronomy. He formulated three important laws of planetary motion to which mathematical equations were added to support mere observation. Galileo, among other things, built a telescope and formulated laws of acceleration and dynamics. He thought that scientific results should consist in mathematically precise laws, so made his physics thoroughly mathematical, famously claiming that 'this grand book, the universe. . .is written in. . .mathematical characters'.[3] In 1632, the Catholic Church censored Galileo's *Dialogue Concerning the Two Chief World Systems* for openly advocating the Copernican theory. The endorsement of the Copernican theory in this work also prompted his trial and condemnation in the following year on a charge of heresy.

Sir Isaac Newton (1642–1727), the legendary English scientist, added to the picture with his own famous laws of motion, not to mention his theory of gravitation, in which he combined Kepler's laws for planetary motion and Galileo's law of falling bodies into the single inverse-square law of gravitational attraction. In his groundbreaking 1687 scientific work, *The Mathematical Principles of Philosophy* (*Philosophiae Naturalis Principia Mathematica*), a system of the world is presented modeled on the geometry of the ancient Greek mathematician Euclid (c. 325 CE–c. CE 265), wherein theorems are derived from axioms and postulates. In accordance with the geometrical style, the first volume of the *Principia* begins with definitions and axioms from which propositions are demonstrated.

Unlike medieval thinkers who proceeded for the most part by reading traditional texts, the early modern scientists laid great stress on observation, experiments and mathematical calculation. Faced with the overwhelming success of the new sciences, Early Modern philosophers aimed to make philosophical knowledge as secure as scientific knowledge. These new scientific modes of thought influenced philosophic thought by giving rise to two models of how we gain our knowledge of the world: empiricism and rationalism.

2.2. EMPIRICISM AND RATIONALISM

The terms 'empiricism' and 'rationalism' can mean many different things. In the present context, these terms refer specifically to the growth of empiricism in the British Isles (sometimes referred to as 'British empiricism') and the rise of rationalism primarily in continental Europe (sometimes referred to as 'Contintental rationalism') during the seventeenth and eighteenth centuries. Major figures in the

empiricist tradition include Francis Bacon (1561–1626), Thomas
Hobbes (1588–1679), Locke, Berkeley and, of course, Hume.
Rationalism originated with Descartes. Other major figures in the
tradition include Malebranche, Benedict (Baruch) Spinoza
(1632–1677), and Gottfried Leibniz (1646–1716).

Empiricists emphasize experience and observation as the primary
source of all knowledge. Bacon is an early example of those who
advocated the experimental and observational method for the acquisition and defense of knowledge. He claimed in *The New Organon*
that our understanding of things extends only so far as to what has
been 'observed of the order of nature', so the first step of inquiry is
to 'elicit the discovery of true causes and axioms from every kind
of experience' supported by 'illuminating. . .experiments'.[4] Locke
thought that all knowledge is founded on experience. Specifically,
the two fountains of knowledge, from which all of our ideas origi-
nate, are sensation and reflection. The former are observations from
our senses about '*external, sensible Objects*', which give rise to ideas
such as sweet or bitter, blue or red, hot or cold, hard or soft etc. The
latter are observations derived from reflection, which are ideas of the
internal operations of our own minds, such as thinking, doubting,
reasoning, believing, and willing (ECHU 2.1.2–4). Berkeley and
Hume mostly agree but with some important modifications.
Berkeley thinks that the 'objects of human knowledge' come from
either (i) ideas from the senses, or (ii) ideas perceived when one
reflects on the 'passions or operations of the mind', or (iii) ideas
formed by the memory and imagination (PHK 1: §1). Hume thought
that the faculties of memory and imagination deal with ideas; ideas
themselves are acquired from impressions of sensation and impressions of reflection (see this volume Chapter 4.1–3).

Whereas the empiricists assign a fundamental role to experience
as the basis of our knowledge claims, philosophers in the rationalist
tradition tend to think that human reason can in fact be the source
of all knowledge about the way the world is, thereby privileging
knowledge gained by reason over knowledge gained by sense experience. Descartes, Malebranche and Spinoza, for instance, all
emphasize that sense experience can be deceptive and unreliable as
a source of knowledge and needs to be aided or corrected by the use
of reason.[5] Unlike empiricism, which begins with observation and
experience as the source of knowledge, rationalism begins with self-
evident truths that form the basis for knowledge. These truths, which

are held to be certain and indubitable, constitute the foundation from which further knowledge is deduced, knowledge which is also held to be certain and indubitable. Rationalist philosophy is more modeled on the example of mathematics as it involves reasoning logically from self-evident truths, in the style exemplified in geometry. Spinoza's *Ethics* epitomizes the geometrical method. Each of the five parts of the *Ethics* begins with numbered axioms and definitions, from which numbered propositions are demonstrated, as well as the occasional corollary.

It is important to note the limitations of this distinction between 'empiricism' and 'rationalism', which was drawn only much later. First, the distinction overlooks the fact that there are important differences in many points amongst individual philosophers classified in the same camp. For example, while both Locke and Berkeley agree that the object of human knowledge is ideas derived from sensation and reflection, many points of disagreement remain between them; in fact, Berkeley wanted to rid Locke's philosophy of the elements deemed inconsistent with empiricism, such as the theory of abstract ideas and the nature of an external world (see Chapter 2.3.5). Second, the distinction tends to underplay the similarities between the philosophers appointed in opposing camps. For instance, both Descartes and Spinoza emphasize the importance of experiments and sensory observation in the attainment of knowledge, and Bacon, Locke and Hume certainly do not reject the role of reason in their philosophies. Hume thought that reason was a very important feature or aspect belonging to the imaginative faculty and comes in two types: demonstrative and probable or moral reasoning (see Chapter 4.3.1).[6]

2.3. MAIN INFLUENCES

On 26th August 1737, shortly after leaving La Flèche where he wrote most of his *Treatise of Human Nature*, Hume wrote a letter to a friend in Britain suggesting four works which would help in understanding the metaphysical parts of his reasoning. The four works are Descartes' *Meditations on First Philosophy*, Malebranche's *The Search After Truth*, Berkeley's *Treatise Concerning the Principles of Human Knowledge* and Bayle's *Historical and Critical Dictionary* (*Dictionaire historique et critique*); of particular interest were articles on Zeno of Elea (c. 495 CE–c. CE 430) and Spinoza. For the sake of completeness, Newton's *Mathematical Principles of Philosophy* and Locke's *Essay Concerning Human Understanding* have been added to the list in the ensuing discussion of Hume's main influences.

2.3.1. Descartes

In his *Meditations on the First Philosophy*, Descartes judged that many of his beliefs might well be false, and documents his quest for true beliefs and certain knowledge. He thought that certain knowledge required a firm and unshakeable foundation. Once the foundation of knowledge is discovered, further knowledge can be inferred from that foundation, thereby acquiring true beliefs that rest on a firm foundation. Playing the role of a sceptic discovers the basis for knowledge. Descartes doubts all those beliefs that can possibly be doubted in order to determine whether there is any belief immune to doubt upon with which a solid structure of knowledge can be constructed. To put it another way: knowledge is put on a secure foundation by doubting our beliefs and that which cannot be doubted will constitute the certain foundation for inferring further knowledge. Descartes then arrives at one indubitable truth, his own existence, and uses this as a foundation for demonstrating knowledge throughout the rest of the *Meditations*, in particular, knowledge of God's existence, the 'real distinction' between the mind and body and the existence of an external world.

Hume was very much concerned with the use of scepticism and was influenced by, and critical of, Descartes' method of doubt. Hume was also very critical of many of the views that Descartes developed, on topics to do with substance (see Chapter 4.3.2), the existence of a vacuum (see Chapter 5.3), causation (see Chapter 7.1) and the immateriality of the soul (see Chapter 8.5).[7] Finally, in his important discussion of why a cause is always necessary, Hume uses the idea that nothing we imagine is absolutely impossible (see Chapter 6.2), borrowing from Descartes' maxim that 'Existence is contained in the idea or concept of every single thing, since we cannot conceive of anything except as existing' (CSM II: 117).

2.3.2. Malebranche

Two aspects of Malebranche's *Search After Truth* were especially influential in Hume's philosophy and these are his doctrines of the vision in God and Occasionalism. The vision in God is the view that we see all things by means of ideas in God. The argument for the position that begins with the claim that it is universally agreed upon that we do not directly perceive external objects, since we see the sun and the stars and it can hardly be the case that 'the soul should leave the body to stroll about the heavens' to see the objects present there (ST 217). What we perceive instead are ideas. The mind's immediate object when it sees the sun is not the sun, but an idea of the sun. Our minds get ideas of external objects because God himself contains ideas of all external things, and He reveals these ideas to our minds at the appropriate time. Hume was influenced by Malebranche's claim that it is only through the presence of ideas that we can perceive material bodies.[8] At *Treatise* 1.2.6 Hume presents a universal principle that 'nothing is ever really present with the mind but its perceptions or impressions and ideas, and that external objects become known to us only by those perceptions they occasion' (THN 1.2.6.7; SBN 67). Since the mind has nothing but perceptions in front of it, even when we focus our attention 'to the heavens, or to the utmost limits of the universe; we never really advance a step beyond ourselves, nor can conceive any kind of existence, but those perceptions' (THN 1.2.6.8; SBN 67). While Hume, like Malebranche, argues for the impossibility of our having any ideas of external existence not of the same kind as our perceptions or ideas, it is important to note that he certainly does not adopt Malebranche's theological conclusion that we see external objects by viewing their images as they reside in God.

The universal principle plays an important part of Hume's system, appearing a total of three times in Book 1 of the *Treatise* (1.2.6.7; 1.4.2.21; 1.4.5.15). The principle also turns up again in Book 2 in his theory of the passions (2.2.2.22), and in his moral theory in Book 3 (3.1.1.2). The principle also appears in the final section on scepticism in *An Enquiry Concerning Human Understanding* (EHU 12.9–16; SBN 152–5). Other philosophers who embraced the universal principle include Antoine Arnauld (1612–1694) and Pierre Nicole (1625–1695), whose discussion of the nature and origin of ideas in *The Art of Thinking* begins with the claim that 'we can have no knowledge of what is outside us except by means of the ideas in us' (AT 25). Hume ranks *The Art of Thinking* as one of 'the common systems of logic' alongside Malebranche's *Search After Truth* and Locke's *Essay Concerning Human Understanding* in the Abstract to the *Treatise*.[9] Locke was a fan of the universal principle also. In the second book of the *Essay* on the origin of ideas, he claims that the mind 'stirs not one jot beyond those *Ideas*, which *Senses* or *Reflection*, have offered for its Contemplation' (ECHU 2.1.24). An idea is defined as the 'immediate object of perception' (ECHU 2.8.8) and 'Since the Mind. . .hath no other immediate Object but its own Ideas, which it alone does or can contemplate, it is evident, that our Knowledge is only conversant about them' (ECHU 4.1.1). It stands to reason that Locke's focus when explaining our knowledge of the existence of external objects is our ideas, as it is the 'actual receiving of *Ideas* from without that gives us notice' of the existence of external things (ECHU 4.11.2).

Malebranche's Occasionalism also influenced Hume. Central to this doctrine is the definition of a 'true cause'. A true cause 'is one such that the mind perceives a necessary connection between it and its effect' (ST 450). The necessary connection is a connection by which the effect must follow necessarily from the cause: the cause necessitates the effect, making it impossible that the effect does not follow. The only thing whose effects follow necessarily from it is an omnipotent (all powerful) will. God is the only being with an omnipotent will, so God is the only true cause. God has to be the only true cause as it is inconceivable that God should will something to occur and for that event not to occur without the other. This means that God is the principal force behind all causal connections between events in the world. For example, when a cricket bat strikes a cricket ball, God is the actual cause of the motion of the ball. The cricket bat is merely the occasional or incidental cause which signals God to actually move the ball. God is also the true cause behind human bodily motion. For example, when I willfully turn on my computer, my will is only the occasional cause, and God is the true cause of the motion. While Hume argued vigorously against Malebranche's theological solution to the problem of causality, his discussion of the nature of a necessary connection between cause and effect is much indebted to Malebranche's formulation of the issue (see Chapter 7.1).[10]

2.3.3. Newton

It is generally thought that Newton's scientific work, *The Mathematical Principles of Philosophy*, greatly influenced the philosophy of the British empiricists,[11] particularly Hume.[12] In particular, it is thought that Hume was influenced by the experimental method utilized by Newton (see Chapter 3.3.1), in addition to Newton's four rules of scientific reasoning outlined in the second volume of the *Mathematical Principles*, which were later adopted in part by Hume in the *Treatise* (see Chapter 6.6). Further, Newton's theory of gravitational attraction in the natural world shaped Hume's talk of an attraction in the mental world (see Chapter 4.3).

There are important differences between these two thinkers however. One difference between their philosophies concerns the nature of space (see Chapter 5.3). Another difference between them concerns theological matters. Newton thought that the discoveries of science provided evidence for belief in God as the first non-mechanical cause responsible for the ultimate origin and continuing order of nature (MP II: 544).[13] His reasoning is a version of the Design Argument. The design, order, harmony of planetary motion, as formulated in the scientific laws of motion and gravity, implies a living, intelligent and powerful creator, God, the first cause. While Hume was certainly interested in and wrote much about the subject matter of religion, he pointedly avoids making theological speculations in his philosophical conclusions. In his famous search for the impression of power or necessary connection in 'Of the Idea of Necessary Connexion' in Section VII of the *Enquiry*, he rejects the 'theory of the universal energy and operations of the Supreme Being' because it carries us beyond sensory experience (see Chapter 7.1). Further, at the end of liberty and necessity in Section VIII of the *Enquiry*, when responding to an objection, he recommends that we avoid uncertainties to do with God as the first cause of the universe. There is also Hume's sustained critique of the design argument in 'Of a Particular Providence and a Future State' (*Enquiry*, Section XI), and in the *Dialogues Concerning Natural Religion*. Indeed, according to some scholars, Hume's critique of the design argument in these works is a direct attack on Newton and his followers.[14]

2.3.4. Locke

Hume places Locke's *Essay Concerning Human Understanding* as one of 'the common systems of logic' alongside Arnauld and Nicole's *The Art of Thinking* and Malebranche's *Search After Truth* and in the Abstract to the *Treatise*.[15] In Book 1 of the *Essay*, Locke prefaces his theory that all ideas are derived from experience with an attack on the doctrine that certain innate principles, such as

'Whatever is, is' and 'The whole is greater than the part', that are 'stamped upon the Mind', which the soul brings into the world with it (ECHU 1.2.1). Locke famously likens the mind to a piece of blank white paper, 'void of all characters, without any ideas'; the mind comes to be furnished with ideas by experience (ECHU 2.1.1–2). Hume shares Locke's fundamental view that the root of all knowledge lies in experience, although he claims that his own distinction between the perceptions of the mind into impressions and ideas is an improvement of what Locke was after in his denial of innate principles in the *Essay* (see Chapter 4.1–3). Both philosophers also intend to discover, in Locke's words, 'the original, certainty, and extent of human knowledge' (ECHU 1.1.2); Hume's science of human nature aims to acquaint us with 'the extent and force of human understanding' (THN Intro. 4; SBN xv).

However, despite sharing a number of beliefs or methods and aims, Locke and Hume draw very different conclusions and positions on many issues. Some examples to be discussed include abstract ideas (see Chapters 2.3.5, 4.4.3), the association of ideas (see Chapter 4.3), substance (see Chapter 4.3.2), the existence of a vacuum (see Chapter 5.3), causation (see Chapter 6.2), power (see Chapter 7.1) and the nature of external objects (see Chapter 8.2–4).

2.3.5. Berkeley

Another work that Hume mentions in the letter is Berkeley's *Principles of Human Knowledge*. In this work, Berkeley defends immaterialism. According to this position, all physical things exist as collections of ideas in the mind that are fed to us directly by God. Physical objects are thus mind-dependent, that is, the existence of them depends on being perceived by us and no such external objects exist apart from our own knowledge or consciousness of them. Berkeley maintains that the existence of things without any relation to their being perceived is not only unintelligible, but impossible – he claims that it is not possible for external objects to have any existence 'out of the minds or thinking things which perceive them' (PHK 1: §3).[16] Although rejecting Berkeley's theological solution, Hume was impressed with Berkeley's arguments showing the difficulties of accessing an external world behind our perceptions; he writes that most of Berkeley's writings 'form the best lessons of scepticism, which are to be found either among the ancient or modern authors, Bayle not excepted' (EHU 12.1.15n; SBN 155n).

Hume was also influenced by Berkeley's critique of the distinction between primary and secondary qualities. This distinction has its roots in Galileo's *The Assayer* and Descartes' Sixth Meditation, but perhaps the most famous expression of this position comes from Locke's *Essay*. He thought that qualities are powers in objects 'to produce ideas in our minds' (ECHU 2.8.8). Primary qualities, powers in objects to produce the ideas of solidity, extension, figure, motion or rest, number, bulk, and texture, are the real, mind-independent parts of objects. Primary qualities are powers in bodies that not only resemble our ideas of them, but also are 'utterly insep-arable from the body in whatever state it is in' (ECHU 2.8.9). Secondary qualities, on the other hand, are the powers in objects to produce ideas of colors, sounds, tastes and smells. These are mind-relative qualities of objects. Our ideas of secondary qualities resem-ble nothing in the object. Our ideas of colors, sounds and so on, do not resemble secondary qualities which are merely powers in the objects to produce such ideas in us of these qualities; nor do such ideas resemble the grounds of these powers, which are the primary qualities of minute particles. Berkeley famously disputed this dis-tinction, arguing that the relativity of the ideas of secondary quali-ties applies equally to primary qualities. Just as the apparent color of an object changes when our perceptual situation changes, so does the apparent size, shape, and so on. Further, bodies cannot be con-ceived as having primary qualities unless they are also conceived as having at least some secondary quality. Hume will have much to say about this distinction (see Chapter 8.2–5).

Finally, Berkeley's theory about abstract ideas is taken over by Hume (see Chapter 4.4.3). Hume claims that Berkeley's theory of abstraction is 'one of the greatest and most valuable discoveries that has been made of late years' (THN 1.1.7.1; SBN 17). The topic of abstract ideas was a major source of dispute between Locke and Berkeley. Locke was concerned to explain how abstract or general ideas are formed out of particular ones, in other words, the way in which a particular idea, such as a person or a cow, comes to stand for a general class of things: persons or cows. He illustrates the process by examples. Children begin with sense impressions of par-ticular individual persons, such as '*Nurse* and *Mamma*' and thereby noticing that many things in the world resemble these individual persons, they frame a general idea of 'person' (ECHU 3.3.7). He goes on to say that in doing so 'they make nothing new, but simply leave out of the complex *Idea* they had of *Peter* and *James*, *Mary* and *Jane*, that which is peculiar to them all and retain what only is common to them all' (ECHU 3.3.7). The process of abstraction consists in our comparing ideas of various particulars encountered in experience, noting their similarities and differences, ignoring the latter and retaining in the mind only the former as a general abstract idea which may be employed in classifying further particulars that we meet.

Berkeley took exception to this in the *Principles Concerning Human Knowledge*. He thought Locke's argument results in the idea of a human that is colored, but not a specific color, that has a size and shape but no determinate size or shape, and so forth (PHK Intro. §§8–9). Berkeley argues that he has never been able, by introspection, to discover any abstract ideas of this nature, claiming that 'the idea of a man that I frame to myself, must be either of a white, or a black, or a tawny, a straight, or a crooked, a tall or a low, or a middle-sized man' (PHK Intro. §10). Second, Berkeley argues that we do not need it because a simpler explanation is available (PHK Intro. §§11–12). Berkeley allows that we can abstract 'in one sense' (PHK Intro. §10). All ideas are particular. A particular idea can be used to represent in a general way, just as a diagram of a particular triangle can be used to represent all triangles or when a geometer draws a line on a blackboard, it is taken to represent all lines, even though the line itself is particular and has determinate qualities. He writes that 'a word becomes general by being made the sign, not of an abstract general idea but, of several particular ideas, any one of which it indifferently suggests to the mind' (PHK Intro. §11). Ideas remain particular, although a particular idea can function as a general idea. Berkeley's final argument turns on Locke's description of the abstract general idea of a triangle, an idea which 'must be neither oblique nor rectangle, neither equilateral, equicrural, nor scalenon, but *all and none* of these at once' (ECHU 4.7.9). Berkeley thinks that the described idea represents an impossible state of affairs, and is therefore inconceivable, since whatever is impossible is inconceivable (PHK Intro. §13).[17]

2.3.6. Bayle
The last work is Bayle's *Dictionary*. Hume cites two particular articles to do with Zeno and Spinoza. Zeno was famous for a series of paradoxes that show the contradictory nature of motion and space.

In his discussion of Zeno's paradoxes, Bayle suggests that if space exists, it must be composed of or made up of one of either: mathematical points, indivisible physical points, or minute and infinitely divisible parts (HD 361). Bayle concludes that all three opinions are absurd. Hume draws on Bayle's discussion of infinite divisibility in his own account of the origin of the ideas of space and time in the second part of Book 1 of the *Treatise* (see Chapter 5.1). However, while Bayle sceptically concludes that none of the three options provide an adequate explanation of space, Hume more positively explains how we get the idea of space, opting for the indivisible points (see Chapter 5.2).

Hume also takes from the article 'Spinoza' the objections Bayle lodged against Spinoza's substance monism: the doctrine that there is only one substance, which is God. What appear to be individual objects, such as rocks, flowers and trees, are in fact only modifications of God's one substance. Bayle famously refers to Spinoza's monism as a 'most monstrous hypothesis', arguing that it is counterintuitive to see all physical things as modifications of a single substance (HD 300). In Book 1, Part 4 of the *Treatise*, Hume extends Bayle's critique to show that the very objections used by theologians against Spinoza's theory of substance apply equally well to the theologians' own theories about the immaterial substance of the soul (see Chapter 8.5). Finally, and more generally, Hume is also supposed to have been influenced by Bayle's historical account of the types of scepticism and his use of sceptical argument in attacking orthodox positions.[18]

2.4. SUMMARY

So far, a survey has been made of some of the main historical forces, such as the growth of science, the emergence of rationalism in Continental Europe and empiricism in the British Isles, in addition to certain intellectual figures that helped shape Hume's thought. The next step is to see how this array of intellectual currents and influences plays out in Hume's system.

Before moving on, it is worth emphasizing that there are undoubtedly many, many other historical currents and figures that helped shape Hume's philosophy apart from those discussed here. It has been wisely remarked by David Fate Norton that 'no single writer or philosophical tradition can be relied on to provide a comprehensive key to his thought'.[19] Hume was a widely read man: at around March 1734, he reported having read most of the celebrated books in English, French, and Latin and he was acquiring the Italian.[20] By the time he left university, he had exposure to classical authors like Cicero (106–43 BCE), Seneca (c. 4 BCE–CE 65), Tacitus (c. CE 56–c. CE 117), Lucretius (c. 99–c. 55 BCE) and Plutarch (c. BCE 46–c. CE 119). His early reading included many English poets and essayists of the period such as John Milton (1608–1674), John Dryden (1631–1700), John Rochester (1647–1680), Matthew Prior (1664–1721), Alexander Pope (1688–1744), Jonathan Swift (1667–1745), Joseph Addison (1672–1716) and Sir Richard Steele (1672–1729). In the Introduction to the *Treatise*, Hume mentions natural philosopher Robert Boyle (1627–1692) and the moral philosophy of Lord Shaftesbury (1671–1713), Francis Hutcheson (1694–1746),[21] Butler and Bernard Mandeville (1670–1733) and during the course of the work he refers to Hobbes, Blaise Pascal (1623–1662) and Samuel Clarke (1675–1729).[22] Other figures impacting his thought include Niccolò Machiavelli (1469–1527), Michel Montaigne (1533–1592), Hugo Grotius (1583–1645), Pierre Gassendi (1592–1655), Nicolas Boileau (1636–1711), Samuel von Pufendorf (1632–1694), Robert Hooke (1635–1703), Baron de Montesquieu (1689–1755) and Henry St. John Bolingbroke (1678–1751).

NOTES

1 For an excellent introduction to modern philosophy, see Thomson (2003), Introduction.
2 This very short discussion of the growth of science is indebted to the editor's introductions in Matthews (1989).
3 In *The Assayer*, see *Discoveries and Opinions of Galileo Galileo* (1959: 237–8). Thanks to Tom Seppalainen for providing this reference.
4 See *The New Organon*, Bacon (2000: 33, 58).
5 See Descartes' First and Sixth Meditations in the *Meditations on First Philosophy*; Book 1 ('The Senses') of Malebranche's *Search After Truth* and Book II, Chapter 1 of Spinoza's *Short Treatise on God, Man and His Well-Being* and the second scholium to Proposition 40 in Part 2 of the *Ethics*.
6 For more on the limitations of the distinction between empiricism and rationalism, see Thomson (2003: 6–7).
7 For a close investigation of the relationship between Hume and Descartes' thought, see Antony Flew (1986), especially chapter 1.
8 Thanks to Brandon Watson for emphasizing this comparison between Malebranche and Hume.

9 See the fourth paragraph in the Abstract to the *Treatise*. Some have even compared Book 1 of Hume's *Treatise* with *The Art of Thinking*. See Hendel's introductory essay in Arnauld and Nicole (1964). For an excellent account of Hume's acquaintance with *The Art of Thinking* and other logic texts, see Charles Echelbarger's 'Hume and the Logicians' in Easton (1977).

10 For a work on Hume that clearly highlights Malebranche's influences, see Wright (1983).

11 Locke considers himself a mere '*underlabourer*' engaged in clearing away some rubble that lies in the path to knowledge in comparison to such masters in an age which includes the '*incomparable Mr*. Newton', and 'his never enough to be admired Book'. See ECHU: The Epistle to the Reader, pp. 9–10; 4.7.3.

12 While it is generally supposed that Hume's philosophy was greatly influenced by Newton's work, some commentators have recently claimed that Newton's influence is far less than has been alleged in Hume scholarship. According to this interpretation, a close reading of his work reveals that he actually knew very little of Newton's work and about science in general, and that his philosophical considerations run counter to Newtonian principles. See particularly Jones (1982), especially pp. 11–19. See also Michael Barfoot, 'Hume and the Culture of Science', in Stewart (1990: 160–1) and Laudan (1981: 84). Elsewhere, I argue that an examination of the method used by Newton and Hume in their philosophy suggests that a more conciliatory approach on the matter is needed. I think there is little doubt that Hume was greatly interested in and influenced by the method outlined in Newton's scientific work, and in science in general. However, I also think that it is prudent not to overemphasize Newton's influence on Hume because there are also some significant differences between their positions when it comes to the application of this method, in particular. See Coventry (2005).

13 See also Newton's *Opticks*, particularly Queries 28 and 31.

14 See Hurlbutt (1963: 135).

15 See the fourth paragraph in the Abstract to the *Treatise*.

16 See also Berkeley (1979).

17 The debate between Locke and Berkeley on abstraction is a matter of some interpretive difficulty. For further reading, see Ayers (1991: chapter 3, 27–8); Dancy (1987: chapter 3); Mackie (1976: chapter 4); Craig (1968: 425–37); Pitcher (1977: chapter 5); and Fogelin (2001: chapters 8–10).

18 See Kemp Smith (1941: chapter 14) for a classic discussion of Bayle's (and Hutcheson's) influence on Hume's thoughts on space and time.

19 See the editors' Introduction to the Norton and Norton edition of the *Treatise*, (2000: 12).

20 See the Introduction to the *Cambridge Companion to Hume* (1993: 2–3).

21 For a thorough investigation of Hutcheson's influence on Hume, see Kemp Smith (1941: Part 1).

22 This list of Hume's influences is drawn from the editors' Introduction to the Norton and Norton edition of the *Treatise* (2000: see p. 12, n.8).

CHAPTER 3

APPROACH TO PHILOSOPHY

The place to begin, as should be the case when tackling any philosophical figure, is to ask, 'What is the writer's view of philosophy?' In other words, what exactly does Hume think that he is doing?

3.1. DEFINITION OF PHILOSOPHY

Hume divides 'philosophy' into two main branches: natural and moral.[1] Natural philosophy concerns the world of spatially extended physical objects and includes what we call now the physical or natural sciences. Hume himself is primarily concerned with moral philosophy or what is sometimes referred to as the 'moral sciences'. The moral sciences relates to the human mind and human life generally and includes what we would now call psychology, human or social sciences, political science, economics, criticism (i.e., of taste, as in 'literary criticism' or 'art criticism', thus including the study of art, poetry, music), in addition to core subjects in philosophy such as religion, ethics, knowledge and logic. Hume also uses the term 'metaphysics' frequently, but not as a term for a distinct subject matter within philosophy to do with the nature of reality as is common practice today, but rather as a term for any difficult or abstract reasoning, regardless of the subject matter.

Hume's most explicit definition of what he takes his own contribution to moral philosophy to be occurs in the conclusion to the *Enquiry Concerning Human Understanding*. Here, he tells us 'philosophical decisions are nothing but the reflections of common life, methodized and corrected' (EHU 12.3.25; SBN 130). There are three important parts to Hume's definition:

- Common life
- Method
- Correction

Hume thinks that philosophical speculation should be relevant to human life and not concerned with fairy tales invented for personal amusement or for hiding our ignorance. Too often philosophy has devised proofs which simply restate our own prejudices or produce scepticism which leads to doubt, confusion and hinders action. Despite all this, one continues to act and engage in the affairs of everyday life. Since we can continue to act in the face of unconvincing proofs and paralyzing doubts, there must be some principles of human thought and action which guide us so we must figure out what these fundamental principles of human nature are.

The distinctive role of philosophy is to methodize these principles of human thought and action and to present them in a clear and understandable fashion, using all the latest scientific advances. Note that Hume thinks that the general principles of the mind can be investigated on a scientific basis. The underlying assumption here is that human beings are part of the order of nature, so they can be examined by the same procedures used in examining the rest of nature.

Finally, philosophy is to have a therapeutic value. Philosophy will better teach human beings how to live with each other by revealing the basic principles of human thought and action. The function of philosophy is to be critical, to expose misconceptions and to help us avoid errors. A 'carefully cultivated' philosophy will help to improve societal affairs, as humans will better succeed in their activities if they clearly understand them. For example, 'The politician will acquire greater foresight and subtility. . .the lawyer more method and finer principles in his reasonings; and the general more regularity in his discipline, and more caution in his plans and operations' (EHU 1.9; SBN 10). Artists will better succeed in their crafts if familiar with accurate knowledge of the operations of the mind and the workings of the emotions (EHU 1.8; SBN 10).

3.2. CHARACTERIZATION OF THE PRESENT STATE OF PHILOSOPHY

Philosophy is in a crisis state, characterized by poor reasoning, endless disputes about every possible issue with no momentous question given any clear answer, and a triumph of eloquence over reason. This is evident even to 'the rabble without doors', who may 'judge from the noise and clamour, which they hear, that all goes not well within' which has given rise to 'that common prejudice against metaphysical reasonings of all kinds' (THN Intro. 2; SBN xiv). People are wary of anything to do with philosophy and the more abstruse or difficult the reasoning involved, the more quickly the line of thought is rejected. Consequently, any metaphysical reasonings or profound philosophical arguments requiring special attention on behalf of the reader are immediately disregarded. People demand that the reasonings brought before them 'at least be natural and entertaining', even if they 'must for ever be a prey to errors and delusions' (THN Intro. 3; SBN xiv).

Hume hopes to correct the disgraceful state of philosophy with a scientific study of the nature of the human mind. He does caution however that the truth cannot be found without hard labour. It would be 'vain and presumptuous' to suppose that the truth can be arrived at 'without pains, while the greatest geniuses have fail'd with the utmost pains' (THN Intro. 3; SBN xiv). In this way, he is preparing us for the intricate arguments to follow.

3.3. THE SCIENCE OF HUMAN NATURE

Hume claims that his anatomy of human nature reconciles two different ways of doing moral philosophy. The first approach sees human beings as active, social creatures, who are influenced by their motives and sentiments. So the philosophical task is to arouse the sentiments of humans by combining lots of 'striking' examples taken from common life with a pleasing literary style, making 'us *feel* the difference between vice and virtue' so they can 'bend our hearts to the love of probity and true honour' (EHU 1.1; SBN 5). This sort of philosophy is popular because it is 'easy and obvious' (EHU 1.3; SBN 6). The second approach emphasizes the rational rather than active parts of our natures, endeavouring 'to form his understanding more than cultivate his manners' and appeals to the reader in its emphasis on rarefied speculation and abstract argument, liable to seem 'unintelligible to common readers' (EHU 1.2; SBN 6). The second sort of philosophy is abstruse and accurate (EHU 1.3; SBN 6).

Hume thought that both approaches capture important aspects of human nature, but that neither tells the whole story. We are both active and reasonable creatures. A view that mixes both styles of philosophy will be best (EHU 1.6; SBN 9). Getting the right mix between popular and abstruse philosophy will not be easy however. The problem with abstruse philosophy is not only that it is 'painful and fatiguing' but also that it is too remote from ordinary life to have any practical application (EHU 1.11; SBN 11). It can indulge the worst excesses of human vanity and is an 'inevitable source of uncertainty and error' because it deals with subjects that are beyond human comprehension (EHU 1.11; SBN 11). Further, the metaphysical arguments are frequently used as a defense or camouflage for popular superstitions, promoting religious fears and prejudices cloaked in profound-sounding but meaningless metaphysical jargon.

The popular philosophy is more useful as it 'enters more into common life', touching the 'hearts and affections' of people thereby reforming conduct (EHU 1.3; SBN 7). The problem however with popular philosophy is that some measure of exact and accurate metaphysical description is needed (EHU 1.8; SBN 9). Delicate sentiment requires just reasoning, and an adequate account of just reasoning requires an accurate and precise metaphysics. The only way to correct sentiment and avoid the sources of error and uncertainty rooted in abstruse philosophy, is to do more metaphysics, but of the right kind. We must pursue *true metaphysics* if we want to jettison these false and deceptive views (EHU 1.12; SBN 12).

The project of true metaphysics is the science of human nature: a serious investigation into the nature of human understanding, in which one stakes out the parts of the mind and discovers the powers and limits of human understanding; engaging in a sort of 'mental geography' (EHU 1.13; SBN 13). This kind of mental geography that constitutes true metaphysics will replace the old incoherent metaphysics with the accurate description of common life that is the proper goal of philosophy. 'Accurate and just reasoning' about human nature will provide an exact picture of the powers and limitations of human understanding and we will see that the capacities of the human understanding are not fit for abstruse or mysterious subjects (EHU 1.12; SBN 12).

The reconciliation between popular and abstruse philosophy, a union of 'profound enquiry with clearness, and truth with novelty', is necessary for three reasons (EHU 1.17; SBN 16). Humans are social and active beings, so they will better succeed in their activities if they clearly understand them. Second, a theoretical inquiry cannot succeed if it is carried on in abstraction from human behavior. Third, when a theory is clearly related to practice we can 'undermine the foundations of an abstruse philosophy which seems to have hitherto served only as a shelter to superstition and a cover to absurdity and error!' (EHU 1.17; SBN 16).

This science of human nature is itself the fundamental science. The science is fundamental because all the other sciences depend on it. He claims that 'all the sciences have a relation, greater or less, to human nature' (THN Intro. 4; SBN xv) and that 'almost all the sciences are comprehended in the science of human nature and are dependent on it' (AB 3; SBN 646). Hume's point is that every other science, logic, morals, criticism, politics, and including natural philosophy, religion and mathematics, is a product of human reasoning, judged by human powers and faculties. Given that 'the science of man is the only solid foundation for the other sciences', the only course of action is 'to march up directly to the capital or center of these sciences, to human nature itself' (THN Intro. 7; SBN xvi). Then we can 'extend our conquests over all those sciences' as 'There is no question of importance, whose decision is not compriz'd in the science of man' (THN Intro. 6; SBN xvi). There is thus a mutual relationship between the science of human nature and the other sciences: not only can the other sciences be used to study human understanding but also the science of human nature can be used to instruct and improve the other sciences.

The method proposed for this study of human nature is partly based on the experimental methods utilized by Newton in the *Principia*. Newton proved the method successful in natural philosophy and now Hume wishes to extend it to the realm of moral philosophy, accordingly, each book of the *Treatise of Human Nature* is subtitled 'Being an attempt to introduce the experimental method of reasoning into moral subjects'. This is why scholars often say things like it was Hume's ambition to be the Newton of the moral sciences or that Hume is the Newton of the science of man.[2] Other thinkers following the experimental method based on human nature are Bacon, Locke, Shaftesbury, Mandeville, Hutcheson, and Butler (THN Intro. 7; SBN xvii; AB 2; SBN 646).

3.3.1. The experimental method
Hume thought that by introducing 'the experimental method of reasoning into moral subjects', philosophy will be put on a 'solid

foundation' of 'experience and observation', in the same manner Newton successfully provided a secure foundation in the natural sciences (THN Intro. 7; SBN xvi; AB 1; SBN 645). There are four similarities between the experimental method advanced in Newton's natural philosophy and taken over by Hume for use in the moral sciences, which may be summed up as follows:

(1) Reliance on experience and observation
(2) Universality
(3) Simplicity
(4) Rejection of occult hypotheses that go beyond experience

In other words, not only do both Newton and Hume hope to render principles as universally as possible, in addition to making explanatory principles as few and as simple as possible, but both also agree that this approach strictly cannot go beyond experience and that any hypothesis which goes beyond experience is to be abandoned immediately.

Newton argued that the results of all deductions concerning nature must be derived from and verified by observation and experiment (MP II: 398–9). Based on these observations and experiments, general conclusions are derived with an eye to explaining all effects from the fewest causes, and 'from particular causes to more general ones, till the argument end in the most general' (OP 404). Further, Newton abides by the maxim, deemed the first rule of reasoning in philosophy, according to which one must be careful 'to admit no more causes in natural things than such as both true and sufficient to explain their appearances' for 'Nature is pleased with simplicity, and affects not the pomp of superfluous causes' (MP II: 398). That is, one should admit as few principles, causes or explanations as are needed to explain the phenomena. Finally, Newton argued that hypothesis, defined as a theory, whether physical or metaphysical, which has no basis in our experience of phenomena, is not to be regarded in experimental philosophy (MP II: 547). The principle of gravitation is not hypothetical in character because gravity is a property manifest in bodies, observable by experimentation (OP 376, 401). However he makes no claim about knowledge of the ultimate nature of gravity. His law of gravitation specifies that the sun acts on the planets, but he refused to say anything about how or why exactly the sun acts on the planets, admitting famously,

'But hitherto I have not been able to discover the cause of those properties of gravity from phenomenon, and I frame no hypothesis' (MP II: 547).

Hume also thinks that one should always rely on experience and observation and 'promises to draw no conclusion but where he is authorized by experience' (AB 2; SBN 646). In the science of human nature, we carefully observe the behavior of men and women in all of their activities, caught up in the ordinary course of their lives, 'Where experiments of this kind are judiciously collected and compar'd, we may hope to establish on them a science' (THN Intro.10; SBN xix). Note that one 'disadvantage' of the application of the method in the moral sciences is that conducting experiments on purpose, with 'premeditation' is impossible (THN Intro. 10; SBN xix).[3] In the case of natural philosophy, 'When I am at a loss to know the effects of one body upon another in any situation, I need only put them in that situation, and observe what results from it' (THN Intro. 10; SBN xix). In the science of human nature, experiments are taken from the observations of the everyday lives of humans, in their 'behaviour in company, in affairs, and in their pleasures' (THN Intro. 10; SBN xix). Hume's experiments are crucial to the science of human nature. Take careful note of them. In the discussion of love and hatred in the second book of the *Treatise*, he offers eight experiments to confirm his position (THN 2.2.2; SBN 332), and his 'proofs' that the passions of fear and hope are mixtures of grief and joy are said to be on par with proofs concerning prism experiments in optics (THN 2.3.9.19; SBN 444).

Second, the method involves explaining as many things as possible in terms of one universal principle. He hopes that his inquiry into 'the mental powers and economy, if prosecuted with. . .caution' will show that 'one operation and principle of the mind depends on another; which again, may be resolved into one more general and universal', thereby making your explanatory principles as few and as simple as possible (EHU 1.15; SBN 14–5; THN Intro. 8; SBN xvii). In fact, he thinks 'the utmost effort of human reason is, to reduce the principles. . .to a greater simplicity, and to resolve the many particular effects into a few general causes' (EHU 4.1.12; SBN 30).[4] Finally, he recommends the rejection of all explanations which go beyond the realm of experience and the avoidance of hypotheses about unseen ultimate entities (THN Intro. 8; SBN xvii; AB 1; SBN 646). Hume speaks approvingly of Newton's cautiousness about making hypotheses about unobservable entities; he writes that Newton 'trod with cautious and therefore the most secure steps, the only road which leads to true philosophy'.[5]

Hume thinks that we stop our enquiry when we reach the most general principle still capable of empirical observation. Anything beyond this that is mere hypothesis or conjecture is useless because it can never be satisfied. Any explanation in any subject matter is subject to the same limitations: all of the arts and sciences ultimately arrive at a first or basic principle beyond which they cannot proceed and none of them can go beyond experience (THN Intro. 10; SBN xviii). No matter what explanation we offer, someone can always ask, 'Why?' Since it is impossible to provide an answer to every 'Why?' question, we must stop somewhere in our explanations and Hume chooses to stop his inquiry when we reach the most general principle capable of empirical observation. Once the reader sees the impossibility of satisfying this desire for explanations beyond experience, the desire should disappear. Hume is warning us that we will find a point beyond which we cannot go and that this will be just fine. Knowing there is much we do not know and cannot know, we will no longer want to know it, while being content with what we do know from the results achieved in the science of human nature, which despite being unable to explain ultimate principles, will still be as helpful in human affairs as he has already argued it is. It has been remarked by Stuart Hampshire that it is this very philosophical attitude that remains as the 'still living element' in Hume's philosophy, an attitude which accepts and submits itself to 'the natural order, the facts of human nature, without anxiety, and therefore without demand for ultimate solutions'.[6]

3.4. SUMMARY

This chapter looked at Hume's definition of philosophy, his opinion of the current state of philosophy and the proposed project of a science of human nature, or 'mental geography', based on the experimental method. We should always be on the lookout for Hume's use of this method throughout his work.

Next, we turn to the three fundamental principles that form the basis of his science of human nature. It is important to get a good grip on the fundamental principles in his system right away as he always relates his arguments to basic principles he establishes at the beginning of his work. Notice that this makes it easier to follow his writing because all of his arguments are based on what he said before. That is why Hume's style of writing rewards the careful reader.

NOTES

1 Here I am drawing from Garrett (1997): 4–5 and the editors' Introduction to the Norton and Norton edition of the *Treatise* (2000: 13, n.11).
2 Capaldi (1975), see Preface and 49, Passmore (1952:43) and Flew (1961: 94). See also Jessop's, 'Some Misunderstandings of Hume', in Chappell (1966: 46–7); P. L. Gardiner, 'Hume's Theory of the Passions', in Pears (1963: 41). See also Stroud (1977: 5).
3 See John Biro's contribution, 'Hume's New Science of the Mind', in the *Cambridge Companion to Hume* (1993: 35).
4 See also THN 3.3.1.10; SBN 578 and the *Dialogues Concerning Natural Religion*, in which Philo claims that 'To multiply causes, without necessity, is indeed contrary to philosophy' (DNR 36).
5 Hume (1885: ch. lxxi).
6 See Hampshire's 'Hume's Place in Philosophy', in *David Hume: A Symposium* (1966: 9–10).

CHAPTER 4

OPERATIONS OF THE MIND

Hume opens his inquiry by outlining the 'elements of this philosophy' (THN 1.1.4.7; SBN 13). The main elements center on three fundamental principles: (1) The Copy Principle (2) The Separability Principle (3) The Principles of the Association of Ideas. All three principles are very important to grasp as one or more of these principles plays a crucial role in his arguments about substance, abstract ideas, space and time, causation, necessity, free will, personal identity and scepticism at one point or another. These general principles of human thought provide also a map of the division of the contents of the human understanding, Hume's 'mental geography' so to speak. The structure of the mind is best illustrated by the following chart:[1]

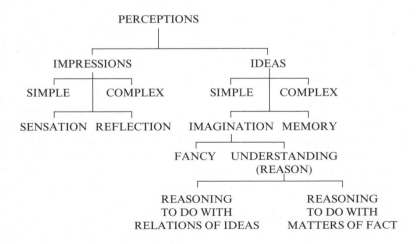

We begin with Hume's division of the perceptions of the mind into impressions and ideas. This distinction is the crux of the first principle to be established in Hume's science of human nature, the Copy Principle, which is the doctrine that 'all our ideas or more feeble perceptions are copies of our impressions or more lively ones' (EHU 2.8; SBN 19; THN 1.1.1.12; SBN 7). This principle is sometimes referred to also as the 'Copy Thesis', the 'Theory of Ideas' or the 'Theory of Meaning'.

4.1. THE COPY PRINCIPLE

As we saw in Chapter 2.2, like Locke, Hume thought that all the contents of the mind are derived from experience, although there are important terminological differences between them. Locke counts all perceptions, including sensations, thoughts and passions, under the term 'ideas', whereas Hume uses the term 'perception' to cover the contents of the mind in general, dividing perceptions into impressions and ideas.[2] Impressions are our more lively perceptions, 'when we hear, or see, or feel, or love, or hate, or desire, or will' and include all our sensations, passions, and emotions (EHU 2.3; SBN 18). Ideas occur in thinking and reasoning and are 'less lively perceptions, of which we are conscious, when we reflect on any of those sensations or movements above mentioned'; ideas are faint images of these impressions (EHU 2.3; SBN 18).

Hume thinks that the difference between impressions and ideas is obvious: there is plainly a difference between the sensation of experience of heat which is an impression and thinking about that sensation of heat at a later time when we are no longer experiencing it, which is an idea. Two further examples that illustrate the difference between impressions and ideas are as follows:

- A person in a fit of anger acts very differently than a person who merely thinks of that same emotion
- A person can easily understand a situation if told about another person who happens to be madly in love, but that same person never can mistake that conception for the actual experience of the electrifying turbulence of that passion (EHU 2.2; SBN 17).

In sum, the difference between impressions and ideas is the difference between feeling and thinking (THN 1.1.1.1; SBN 2; AB 5; SBN 647).

Notice that ideas and impressions differ in terms of liveliness, particularly 'their degree of force and vivacity' (THN 1.1.1.3; SBN 2). Impressions enter into our minds with the most force and are much more vivid, and violent than ideas. Look at a color under normal lighting or in sunlight. Then go to a dark room or to close your eyes and imagine or form a mental image of that color. The actual sensation of the color is more vivid than trying to remember or imagine a color, so the impression of the color is simply more vivid than the idea of the color.

Hume admits exceptions to the doctrine that impressions are more vivid than ideas. In some instances such as sleep, fever and madness, or a highly charged emotional state, it is possible for our ideas to approach the force of the impressions, and sometimes 'our impressions are so faint and low that we cannot distinguish them from our ideas' (THN 1.1.1.1; SBN 1). Nevertheless, he describes these as rare instances that do not alter his doctrine as there is still enough of a difference between impressions and ideas to warrant making the general distinction.

Impressions and ideas can also be simple or complex. Simple ideas or impressions admit of no distinction or separation – this means that they cannot be broken down or be analysed any further. A simple impression would be any impression of sight, smell, taste, sound, touch, or pleasure or pain considered by itself. Simple ideas exactly resemble simple impressions, such as the idea of a shade of color, say of blue or red.

Complex ideas or impressions may be divided into parts. A complex impression is composed of a group of simple impressions. For example, an apple would appear as a complex impression. We see that an apple has a particular color, a certain taste and a certain odour. Color is not the same thing as taste and taste is not the same thing as odor. An apple is capable of being subdivided and having its parts separated into further distinctions.

There is a puzzle though. He observes that many complex ideas never had impressions that correspond to them and many of our complex impressions are never exactly copied in ideas. Hume says that he can imagine a city such as New Jerusalem, even though he has never seen it. He also has an idea of Paris, which he had already visited, but it is certainly not the case that his idea is a perfect representation of all the streets and houses 'in their exact position and proportions' (THN 1.1.1.4; SBN 3).

This puzzle is overcome by recognizing that the Copy Principle applies only to simple impressions and ideas, not to complex ones. So, while complex ideas do not exactly represent or copy complex impressions, complex ideas may be divided into parts or a group of simple ideas which do exactly represent or copy a group of simple impressions. Without exception for every simple idea, there is a corresponding simple impression, and for every simple impression a correspondent idea. Those who deny the universal resemblance are challenged to produce a simple impression that does not have a correspondent idea or a simple idea that does not have the correspondent impression (THN 1.1.1.5; SBN 4; EHU 2–6; SBN 19–20). Hume thus establishes as a 'general proposition' that 'all our simple ideas in their first appearance are deriv'd from simple impressions, which are correspondent to them, and which they exactly represent' (THN 1.1.1.7; SBN 4).[3] That is, for any idea we select, we can trace ultimately the component parts of that idea to impressions rooted in some external sensation or internal feeling. This is the case even with the idea of God as an infinitely wise, intelligent and good Being, which arises from reflecting on the operations of our minds and augmenting without limit the qualities of goodness and wisdom (EHU 2.6; SBN 19–20).

The Copy Principle is very important for the science of human nature. Hume uses the principle to discard metaphysical jargon that has drawn disgrace on philosophy (EHU 2.9; SBN 21). Philosophers often use terms which possess no definitive meaning. If there is suspicion that a word has been used without a clear meaning, all you need to do is properly apply the Copy Principle and ask from what impression the supposed idea derives. If it is impossible to assign any, this will serve to confirm our suspicion that the term is meaningless (EHU 2.9; SBN 22; AB 7; SBN 648–9). Hume will ask from what impression the idea of substance is derived? He does the same in the case of the personal identity, space and time and in the case of a necessary connection between cause and effect. The Copy Principle is also used to defend his analysis of abstract ideas.

4.1.1. Two examples in support of the Copy Principle
The two examples that Hume offers are meant to show that impressions are prior to ideas. Impressions appear first, whereas ideas appear only after we have had impressions. Consider:

- If you want to teach a child the idea of the color blue or the taste of sweetness, you present the actual objects to produce the impressions, rather than producing the impressions by attempting to excite the ideas first (THN 1.1.1.8; SBN 5).
- Wherever there is a defect with the faculties (such as if one is born blind or deaf), or if the organ of sensation which gives rise to the impressions has not been put into use, such as if one has never tasted pineapple, the impressions and their correspondent ideas are lost (EHU 2.7; SBN 20; THN 1.1.1.9; SBN 5).

Experience thus teaches that simple impressions always precede corresponding ideas.

4.1.2. The case of the missing shade of blue

There is an exception to the doctrine that impressions are prior to ideas. In the famous case of the missing shade of blue, we are supposed to imagine that a person, who has enjoyed good sight for thirty odd years, has familiarity with colors of all kinds, except on particular shade of blue. If that person is presented with a graded series of blues, running from the deepest to the lightest and if a particular shade of blue which he or she has never seen is absent, he or she will notice a blank in the continuous series and will be able to raise the idea of the particular shade. Hume admits the exception but does not think it is important enough to warrant any change in the general maxim because it is an instance that is 'particular or singular' (THN 1.1.1.10; SBN 6; EHU 2.7; SBN 20).

There are two approaches to Hume's famous mention of the missing shade of blue as a counterexample. The first approach takes the counterexample not to be a serious problem for Hume's Copy Principle. The second approach regards it as a very serious problem. Defenders of the latter approach are puzzled, and at times outraged, about Hume's offhand admission of the counterexample. Some think that in doing so he completely destroys the generality of the principle. Antony Flew takes this position. He thinks that Hume's admission of the counterexample is 'scandalous' and that 'any universal generalization is decisively falsified by even one single genuine counterexample'.[4] Bennett agrees, taking the position that, 'as soon as [Hume] admits the copy thesis is false, and that ideas can be formed in at least one other way, the game is up'.[5] It has also been pointed out that this counterexample is certainly not a particular and singular instance because we could analogously raise instances of a missing tone or taste or smell, or temperature, and even of missing shades of every color.[6]

Other commentators think that Hume can easily deal with the counterexample through other means. He could have argued that the imaginative construction of the missing shade of blue really produces a complex idea.[7] If Hume treats ideas of shades of color as complex rather than simple, then this would not be an exception to the principle that simple ideas are derived from correspondent simple impressions. There is good reason to suppose that Hume could not have plausibly treated ideas of shades of colors as complex however. Paul Stanistreet, for example, argues that the reason why the shade of blue cannot be complex concerns the Separability Principle, in which Hume insists on the imagination's ability to separate different or distinguishable ideas (see Chapter 4.2). If the idea of the missing shade of blue were complex, it would be possible to separate and distinguish its parts, but the difficulty with treating shades of color as complex lies in the impossibility of distinguishing among its supposed parts; a shade of color cannot be analysed any further, so it must be a simple idea.[8]

Stroud points out that the example of the missing shade of blue is 'hypothetical' and that 'there is no suggestion that anyone actually ever has been, or ever will be, in that position'.[9] Now since Hume's Copy Principle is an empirical, contingent generalization,[10] the counterexample is only worrisome if you want to prove that it is 'absolutely impossible' for Hume's thesis to be false. Furthermore, if it turns out that 'the possible exceptions were. . .rare and special, one might be fully justified in ignoring them and basing one's scientific investigations on the general principle'.[11] It might even be possible 'to explain how [the exceptions] could occur without having to invoke any general principles that are not part of, or in line with, Hume's theory of the mind'.[12] Garrett offers just such an explanation. He offers a sophisticated account as to how the idea of missing shade of blue may be obtained without a corresponding simple impression that is intended to show how the case of the missing shade of blue may be admitted without fatally undermining the general usefulness of the principle.[13] The explanation relies on the existence of natural resemblances among simple perceptions.[14] The subject has a large number of simple impressions that naturally resemble the missing impression very closely and are even arranged in such an order that as to point to the content of the missing impression. The operation of the mind uses an array of resembling shades to fill in the blank within an ordering of simple ideas. The missing shade of blue need not be derived from an exactly corresponding impression, although it is derived from a set of closely resembling impressions.

Garrett notes that the process is similar to a phenomenon that occurs with certain passions described by Hume in Book II of the *Treatise*:

> Ideas may be compar'd to the extension and solidity of matter, and impressions, especially reflective ones, to colours, tastes, smells and other sensible qualities. Ideas never admit of a total union, but are endow'd with a kind of impenetrability, by which they exclude each other, and are capable of forming a compound by their conjunction, not by their mixture. On the other hand, impressions and passions are susceptible of an entire union; and like colours, may be blended so perfectly together, that each of them may lose itself, and contribute only to vary that uniform impression, which arises from the whole (THN 2.2.6.1; SBN 366).

In these cases, two simple impressions or two simple passions are imaginatively blended to form a third simple impression or passion. It seems plausible to think, Garrett suggests, that one's ideas of two shades of (say) blue could also be blended to produce a third simple idea, an idea of the missing shade of blue. The case of the missing shade of blue, according to Garrett, 'constitutes a very near miss for the Copy Principle', 'requiring at most a very slight and understandable amendment to Hume's general description of the powers of the imagination'.[15] He concludes that the missing shade of blue 'has little effect on Hume's philosophical uses of the principle', 'because of its special explanations and near-miss character'.[16]

Garrett's solution harmonizes well with Hume's workings of the mind, but lingering reservations may remain. One might still reasonably wonder why Hume was so dismissive of the counterexample; in other words, if he does have a decent solution here that has little effect on the way he wants to use the Copy Principle, then why doesn't he tell us more about it? Why does he move on so quickly? Stroud expresses the misgiving here nicely, finding still Hume's 'rather cavalier attitude towards the exception. . .unsettling'.[17]

Bennett suggests that Hume is so dismissive of the counter-example because 'he. . .realized it does not seriously impede anything he wants to do with the copy thesis'.[18] More properly, I think that to set aside completely concerns about Hume's offhand admission of the counterexample, it is important to remember the difference between the experiments carried out in natural sciences versus those conducted in the moral sciences. The experiments in the science of human nature are taken from the observations of the lives of humans as they go about the ordinary course of their lives, in contrast to the purposeful and premeditated experiments in natural philosophy (THN Intro. 10; SBN xix). Hume need not worry therefore about the possibility of there being some situation, like the missing shade of blue, under which the Copy Principle could break down, so long as that situation is remote from the sort of situations that we actually need to consider in the science of human nature. The science of human nature examines how the human mind naturally operates in everyday life. If Hume's task is to analyze the natural workings of the mind, then the example comes off as highly artificial and irrelevant to the scope of the present investigation. As Stroud points out, the example is a hypothetical one and there is no suggestion that anyone actually ever has been, or ever will be, in that position, so we cannot ever be sure the counterexample had actually occurred in real life. Hume's principle is supposed to cover all ordinary cases of the mind's operations drawn from careful observations of everyday life. Given the restriction on the sorts of the experiments carried out in the science of the mind then, Hume is justified in promptly sidestepping the example, as cases like the missing shade of blue are artificial examples that occur outside his current field of study: the natural operations of the mind.

4.1.3. Impressions and ideas further classified

Hume offers another distinction within the class of impressions and within the class of ideas. Impressions are divided into two kinds: sensation and reflection. Impressions of sensation come to be through our sensory organs, either internal or external, and arise originally 'from unknown causes'; the examination of sensations is not relevant as the subject of sensations belongs more to the anatomists and natural philosophers rather than the moral philosophers (THN 1.1.2.1; SBN 7–8).

Impressions of reflection are derived from our ideas, so they are relevant to the present inquiry. Impressions of reflection include the passions, desires and emotions. These impressions arise from ideas in the following manner. After we have had an impression of pleasure or pain, the mind forms a copy of the impression. This copy is an idea. When the mind recalls the idea, a new impression of desire or aversion is produced. For example, I receive a pleasant sensation when eating chocolate. When I remember the pleasant impression and this memory is now an idea, I have a desire for more chocolate. This desire is a new impression. Nevertheless, I still had the original impression of pleasure. Hume returns to a detailed discussion of these impressions of reflection in Book II of the *Treatise*, 'Of the Passions'.

Ideas are divided between those produced by the memory and those produced by the imagination. When the mind has received impressions, they can reappear to the mind as an idea in one of two ways. First, they may reappear with a degree of vividness which is intermediate between the vividness of an impression and the faintness of an idea. The faculty by which we repeat our impressions in this way is the memory. Second, they can lose their vivacity completely and reappear as ideas, as faint copies of impressions. The faculty by which we repeat our impressions in this way is the imagination (THN 1.1.3.1; SBN 8–9).

Ideas as they appear in the memory have two characteristics. First, the ideas of the memory retain some of the original vivacity of the impressions. This is a fairly common occurrence as when we speak of good and bad memories in order to emphasize that our memories still make us feel pain or pleasure to a certain degree. Second, the primary function of the memory is to preserve the order and position of the original impressions. Accordingly, when we retell a story about something that happened to us in the past, we usually tell it in the order that it happened.

Ideas as they appear in the imagination have the opposite characteristics. Ideas of the imagination have lost all of their original vivacity, so ideas in the memory in contrast are much more lively and strong (THN 1.1.3.1; SBN 9; 1.3.5.3–5; SBN 85). Further, whereas the memory preserves the 'original form' in which the objects presented themselves, the imagination is not tied down in this respect, and is capable of transposing and changing its ideas as much as it pleases (THN 1.1.4.3; SBN 9). Consider, for example, the inventive descriptions of nature in the fables of poems and romances, with its mentions of things like winged horses, fiery dragons, and monstrous giants (THN 1.1.4.5; SBN 10). I have never seen a winged horse. Nevertheless, I have seen plenty of horses, witnessed many kinds of wings on a variety of animals, flying birds and so on. Our imagination combines separate elements from different experiences to create a new creature, like a winged horse, a combination of the idea of a horse with the idea of wings, or to invent a new object, such as a golden mountain, a combination of the idea of gold and the idea of a mountain (EHU 2.5; SBN 19).

4.2. THE SEPARABILITY PRINCIPLE

The Separability Principle is the second principle to be established in the science of the mind. The first full statement of the principle is as follows:

> We have observ'd, that whatever objects are different are distinguishable, and that whatever objects are distinguishable are separable by the thought and imagination. And we may here add, that these propositions are equally true in the *inverse*, and that whatever objects are separable are also distinguishable, and that whatever objects are distinguishable are also different (THN 1.1.7.3; SBN 18).

In sum, Hume thinks that anything the imagination finds distinguishable is capable of existing separately or anything capable of existing separately is distinguishable by the imagination.

This principle is a corollary of the liberty of the imagination to transpose and change its ideas. The imagination is a faculty that breaks apart and recombines ideas, thereby forming new ones. This ability of the imagination is only natural given the fact that all ideas are derived from impressions and 'that there are not any two impressions which are perfectly inseparable' (THN 1.1.3.4; SBN 10). This principle also results from the distinction between simple and complex ideas. An evident consequence of the division into simple and complex is that the components of complex ideas are separable into simple elements, which are then eligible for recombination by the imagination. Simple ideas admit of no distinction, complex ones may be distinguished into parts, so, wherever a difference among ideas is perceived, the imagination can make a separation (THN 1.1.3.4; SBN 10).

This liberty of the imagination turns out to be very important, for Hume uses its corollary, that the mind can separate any ideas it can distinguish, quite often throughout his philosophy on topics such as abstract ideas, space and time, personal identity and causation. There is, however, no explicit statement of the Separability Principle in the *Enquiry*, although a hint of the principle occurs in Section 4 in his discussion of the causal relation. During the course of his argument that all relations of cause and effect are based on experience and not reason, he implies the principle stating that 'every effect is a distinct event from its cause' (EHU 4.11; SBN 30). A probable reason for the omission of the Separability Principle in the *Enquiry* is that most of the topics for which the principle is used for in the *Treatise*, such as abstract ideas, space and time and personal identity, are no longer present in the *Enquiry*.

4.3. PRINCIPLES OF THE ASSOCIATION OF IDEAS

Although the imagination is free to combine ideas as it pleases, it generally works according to three universal Principles of Association by which one idea naturally introduces another. This association of ideas is a psychological mechanism in the imagination, consisting of three bonds of union or ties – resemblance, contiguity, and causation – which unite our ideas together on a regular basis. Because of these three relations, the mind passes naturally from one idea to another. The uniting Principles of Association should not be considered as an 'inseparable connexion' amongst ideas, however, but rather as a 'gentle force' connecting our ideas (THN 1.1.4.1; SBN 10; 1.3.6.13; SBN 92).[19] The gentle force is compared to the force of gravitational attraction. Just as Newton's law of universal gravitation accounts for the movement and subsequent position of all physical particles in the universe, so the Principles of the Association of Ideas will account for every psychological phenomena by explaining how and why various perceptions come to be present in the mind. Another possible influence on Hume here is Hobbes, who devoted a whole chapter in the *Leviathan* to what he calls 'the Consequence or Train of Imaginations' which is the 'succession of one thought to another'.[20]

Hume denies that we can have any knowledge as to the causes of this attraction in the mind (THN 1.1.4.6; SBN 12–3). When we raise the question of what causes the imagination to associate ideas in this way, Hume says that he does not know. Here he invokes the fourth part of the experimental method, the rejection of hypotheses beyond experience. What we can be content with however is an established empirical fact that the imagination really does operate according to these general principles of association and we can leave aside unfruitful speculation about why these principles hold.

These Principles of Association enter into 'most of his philosophy' and he claims that it is his use of the association of ideas which gives him the title of inventor (AB 35; SBN 662). He thinks association helps explain the workings of the mind. He argues that, 'many operations of the human mind depend on the connexion or association' (EHU 3.18), making resemblance, contiguity, and cause and effect 'really *to us* the cement of the universe' (AB 35; SBN 662). This is quite unlike Locke's own position on the matter. Locke devotes a whole chapter on the association of ideas in the *Essay Concerning Human Understanding*, insisting that it is 'a sort of madness' (ECHU 2.33.3). Some examples to illustrate the negative effects of the association of ideas include: children who dislike the dark because their nursemaids have told them stories of goblins or sprites that fill it; people who dislike a perfectly good book because they were once forced under threat of punishment to read it (ECHU 2.33.10, 15). A person will avoid a room, or building or town where something unpleasant to him or her once occurred (ECHU 2.33.11, 15). Hume was well aware of the negative effects of the association of ideas and certainly thinks that these sorts of connections ought to be regulated; however, he also believes that some united ideas in the imagination represent good reasoning (see Chapter 4.3.1).

Hume gives us illustrations of the way in which the mind is moved by these principles. The first principle of association is resemblance. The imagination has a natural tendency to find resemblances of all kinds amongst its ideas. A picture naturally leads our thoughts to the original. So, viewing a photograph of your mother will naturally lead your thoughts to your actual mother.

The second principle is contiguity in time and place. Here, the imagination has a tendency to unite ideas which are derived from impressions which occur close to each other in time and place: the mention of one apartment in a building naturally introduces an enquiry concerning the others; when St. Denis is mentioned, the idea of Paris naturally occurs (AB 35; SBN 662).

The third principle is cause and effect. This is the most extensive relation and produces a strong connection in the imagination (THN 1.1.4.2; SBN 11). Hume's examples of the associative effect of causation are as follows: if we think of a wound, we can 'scarcely forbear' thinking about the pain which follows it (EHU 3.3; SBN 24) and, when we think of the son, we are apt to carry our attention to the father (AB 35; SBN 662). In fact, all relations of blood depend on cause and effect (THN 1.1.4.3; SBN 11–2). Two objects may be considered as placed in this relation when one is the cause of any of the actions or existence of the other or when it has the power of producing it. So for example we might say that 'A master. . .has a power of directing in certain particulars the actions of [a] servant' and that 'A judge is one, who in all disputed cases can fix by his opinion the possession or property of any thing betwixt any members of society' (THN 1.1.4.5; SBN 12). In these cases, all that is required to put the power into action is an exertion of the will on behalf of the master or judge. In Book III of the *Treatise*, 'Of Morals', he points out that the association of cause and effect determines questions of duty, law and morality.

Hume thinks that these Principles of the Association of Ideas explain how most of our beliefs, feelings, and ideas are formed as they show how one thing reminds us of another. He uses the principles in the case of substance, general ideas, space and time, belief, causation, external objects and the self in an attempt to explain how we arrive at such beliefs. Complex ideas are one of the effects of these associations between our ideas. Following Locke's classification in the *Essay* (ECHU 2.12.3–7), Hume divides complex ideas into relations, mode and substance.

4.3.1. Relations

The connection between ideas of the imagination is further divided between two categories or faculties: the fancy and the understanding. Flights of the fancy are representative of some imaginative ideas and these ideas are the source of fantasies, superstitions, and bad philosophy. These sorts of associations between ideas are perhaps the ones that Locke so heartily disapproved of. Hume thinks, however, that other imaginative ideas represent solid reasoning. These ideas are derived from understanding. By the understanding, Hume means that part of the mind which reasons. The objects of reason are divided into two kinds: reasoning concerning relations of ideas (yielding demonstrative, intuitive and certain knowledge) or reasoning about matters of fact (yielding judgments of probability).

Note Hume's special conception of the imagination. Traditionally, the imagination has been thought of as fanciful, irregular and the cause of mistakes. Hume accepts that the imagination may have these characteristics at times. On the other hand, he maintains that the imagination operates according to certain principles which are the only principles for guiding thought and action. Hume gives a new, central role to the imagination.

When we imaginatively exercise our understanding, our minds are guided by seven philosophical or 'reasoning' relations which are divided as follows: resemblance, identity, space and time, quantity or number, quality or degree, contrariety, and causes or effects.[21] These seven different kinds of philosophical relations may be divided into those which depend entirely on the ideas which are being compared and which remain the same as long as the ideas are unchanged, and those which may change without change in the ideas or the objects due to change in location, perspective, and so on. The first category concerns principles of reasoning concerning relations of ideas and includes resemblance, contrariety, degrees in quality, and proportions in quantity or number. The second category concerns principles of reasoning concerning matters of fact and includes identity, relations in time and place, and causation. The topic of relations is delayed until Chapter 6.1.

4.3.2. Substance and mode

A popular topic for discussion was that of substance and mode during Hume's time. Descartes, Malebranche, Spinoza, Leibniz, Locke and Berkeley were all interested in it, although concern for substances can be traced back to at least Aristotle (384–322 BCE).

Substance and mode was a major part of Descartes' metaphysics. In *Principles of Philosophy* I.51, he distinguishes two senses of word substance (CSM I: 210). According to the first sense, substance is that which can exist independently of any other thing. The only substance properly so-called, that is, the only thing that does not depend on anything else for its existence, is God. The second sense concerns created substances of which there are two types: bodies, which possess the principle attribute of extension, and minds, which possess the principal attribute of thinking. Both thinking and extended substances depend on the 'concurrence of God in order to

exist' (CSM I: 210). For Descartes, modes are non-essential properties which cannot be conceived without substance, but without
which substance and its principle attribute can be conceived. Modes
are particular ways of being extended or thinking, that is, particular
sizes, colors, shapes, or particular thoughts, imaginings, or willing a
series of particular acts (CSM I: 211).

In Part 1 of the *Ethics*, Spinoza opts for only one sense of the
word substance. A substance must not only exist in itself, it must also
be conceived through itself, meaning that substance does not
causally depend on anything else for its existence, nor does it need
to be explained thought anything else: understanding substance
does not require knowledge of anything else. There is just one substance and this substance is God. Substance has two attributes:
extension and thought. Modes are ways of having the principle
attributes, particular versions of extension, having a particular
shape, color, size, or particular ways of thinking, judging, hoping,
imagining, or having sensations, etc. All modes are in God and conceived through God.

While Leibniz and Berkeley decide on the existence of only purely
mental or thinking substance, Locke thinks we have two conceptions
of substance. One is a 'notion of pure substance in general' (ECHU
2.23.2), the other 'ideas of particular sorts of substance' (ECHU
2.23.3). According to the first conception, substance in general is
that part of an individual thing in which qualities or properties
inhere. The idea is, we cannot have just qualities, the qualities have
to be attached to something, there must be something which supports them, a substance which contains all of these qualities, even
though the substance itself is not visible. Since we can only observe
a thing's properties, the substance is unknowable. Locke famously
declares that the idea of substance in general is something-he-
knows-not-what that holds together qualities and that it is impossible to discern the relation between the qualities observed and the
substance, which is unknowable except by the qualities (ECHU
1.4.18). The idea of substance is 'nothing, but the supposed, but
unknown support of those Qualities, we find existing, which we
imagine cannot subsist, *sine re substante*, without something to
support them, we call that Support *Substantia*' (ECHU 2.23.2). Our
efforts to speak more positively of substance-in-general are like
those of children when they seek to explain what they do not understand (ECHU 2.23.2). Or we are in the position of Locke's example

of the Indian, who 'saying that the world was supported by a great Elephant, was asked what the Elephant rested on? To which his answer was, A great Tortoise: But being again pressed to know what gave support to the broad-back'd Tortoise, replied, something, he knew not what' (ECHU 2.23.2).

According to the second conception of substance, ideas of substance are combinations of simple ideas taken to represent particular things existing by themselves (ECHU 2.12.6). There are two ideas of this second conception of substance. First, we have ideas of singular substances, for example of a person, or a sheep. Collective ideas of substances are several ideas of these put together, an army of people, or a flock of sheep. Modes are complex ideas which cannot exist by themselves but would be real only if exemplified in a substance; the ideas signified by the words triangle, gratitude and murder (ECHU 2.12.4). There are two types of modes, simple and mixed. Simple modes are constructed by compounding many times the same simple idea without the mixture of any other. One example is number. Suppose that we have a simple idea of the number one, we can repeat this idea or combine three ideas of the same kind to form the complex idea of three, which is a simple mode of one. Other examples include space, duration, infinity, color, taste, smell, and modes of motion and sound. To leap or run are different modifications of motion and, blue and purple are different modifications of color. Mixed modes, like beauty, obligation or theft, are compounded of simple ideas of several kinds (i.e., simple ideas which are not of the same kind) put together to form a complex one. Beauty for example is a combination of color and figure, which causes pleasure in the observer (ECHU 2.12.5).

Hume is suspicious about all this talk of substance, so he applies the Copy Principle to the case. He asks if the idea of substance is derived from an impression of sensation or an impression of reflection? It cannot be derived from impressions of sensation. If perceived by the eyes, it must be a color, if by the ears a sound, if by the palate, a taste. However, no philosopher in favor of substance wants to say that substance is a color, sound or taste. Since it is admitted that we never actually see substance, Hume concludes that we have no impression of sensation corresponding to the idea of substance. The impressions of reflection include passions and emotions and it is obvious that substance is not a passion or emotion. The idea of substance is derived therefore neither from impressions of sensation nor from impressions of reflection. We have no impression of substance, it follows then that there is no idea of substance.

The idea of substance 'is nothing but a collection of simple ideas, that are united by the imagination, and have a particular name assigned them, by which we are able to recall, either to ourselves or others, that collection' (THN 1.1.6.2; SBN 16). Sometimes the particular qualities which form a substance are referred to an unknown something in which they are thought to inhere, but to avoid this 'fiction', the qualities are at least supposed to be closely related with one another by the uniting principles of contiguity and causation. Thus, an association of ideas is set up in the mind and when we discover a new quality of a given substance, the new idea enters into the cluster of associated ideas. Gold is a name that we give to a particular collection of qualities such as a yellow color, a certain weight, malleability, fusibility and when we learn of the fact that it dissolves in *aqua regia*, a type of acid, we then add this quality to the collection of other qualities. In sum, our idea of substance is a collection of simple ideas which the imagination associates with one another on the basis of contiguity and causation. This association is flexible: we may add or subtract an idea here and there while still calling it the same 'substance'.

The idea of a mode is 'a collection of simple ideas' (THN 1.1.6.2; SBN 16). The way they differ from substance is not that they depend on substances, as earlier philosophers had thought. Modes have no principle of association and do not admit of addition or subtraction, as do substances. This may be because the simple ideas making up the mode is distributed among many things, like an activity such as a dance, so that there is no relation of contiguity and causation as there is with substance. If the simple ideas making up the mode are in one thing, such as the quality of beauty in a composition or a painting, what unites them as beautiful 'is not regarded as the foundation of the complex idea' (THN 1.1.6.3; SBN 17). If a new idea is added, you change the mode.

4.3.3. Abstract ideas
A final part of Hume's mental machinery is abstract or general ideas. This account of general terms plays a crucial role in his philosophy, figuring into his views about space and time, necessary connections, aesthetics and morals (see Chapters 5 and 7).

In the *Treatise*, Hume borrows from Berkeley's assertion that abstract or 'general ideas are nothing but particular ones annexed to a certain term which gives them a more extensive signification and makes them recall other individuals which are similar to them' (THN 1.1.7.1; SBN 17). Like Berkeley, Hume denied the human mind's ability to create abstract general ideas of the type claimed by Locke (see Chapter 2.3.5). His own argument concerns the proposition *'that the mind cannot form any notion of quantity or quality without forming a precise notion of the degrees of each'* (THN 1.1.7.3; SBN 18). The lack of a precise common degree to all things falling under a general term produces a dilemma. An abstract general idea must either represent all variants of itself or represent none of its variants. The first alternative is dismissed at once on the ground that the unlimited number of variants implies an infinite capacity in the mind, which Hume regards as impossible (see Chapter 5.1). The second alternative is rejected because Hume holds it to be impossible that there be abstract general ideas with no degrees of quantity or quality, and that if all impressions are completely specific in quantity or quality, the same must be true of ideas. A particular degree of a quality or quantity is a perfectly determinate quality or amount. Hume points out that things falling under the same general term do not have to be exactly alike in any respect, they do not have any perfect determinate quality in common.

With respect to the proposition that the mind cannot form any notion of quantity or quality without forming a precise notion of the degrees of each, Hume gives three arguments. The first depends on the Separability Principle. He observes that whatever objects are separable are distinguishable, and whatever objects are distinguishable are different. Thus, if abstraction is possible, there must be something different and distinguishable to abstract. However, the precise length of line is not different or distinguishable from the line itself, or the precise degree of any quality or quantity. Lines can be of all different lengths, but the length of a particular line is not something distinguishable from the line itself, hence it is not something from which we can abstract to get the general idea of a line. We cannot form a general idea of a line without any length at all, nor can we form a general idea of a line possessing all possible lengths: 'these ideas admit no more of separation than they do of distinction and difference' (THN 1.1.7.3; SBN 19). To take another example, there are many shades of red. A particular red object must have a precise shade of red. Hume's point is that it does not have a color quality different and distinguishable from its precise shade, which it shares with red objects of other shades. We cannot abstract away from the precise shade of color to something common to all red objects because things do not have color qualities distinct from their precise shades.

The second argument turns on the Copy Principle. All ideas are derived from impressions. Every impression is determinate and definite and ideas are as completely determinate as impressions. Since an idea is a copy of an impression, the idea must itself be determinate and definite even though it is fainter than the impression from which it is derived. He believes that it is a contradiction in terms, implying that it is possible for the same thing both to be and not to be, to say that an impression or an idea has no particular degree or proportion.

Hume's third argument starts from the generally received principle that everything in nature is individual and that it is a logical absurdity for a triangle to exist that is not precisely determinate in sides and angles. No triangle can exist which is not a particular triangle with particular characteristics. To postulate an existent triangle which is at the same time all and once every possible kind and size of triangles would be an absurdity. But what is absurd is fact and reality is absurd also in ideas. For, nothing of which there can be a clear and distinct idea can be absurd in fact and reality.

Hume's theory of abstract ideas takes place in terms of what does happen in the mind, drawing upon on his principles of association. In daily experience, one notices that a number of particular objects resemble one another in a particular respect and a habit or custom of applying a term to all of them, notwithstanding their differences, is formed. For example, noticing a certain resemblance among a number of shapes, one calls them all 'triangles'. The term is directly associated with the idea of a particular instance. After you have learnt the word, the idea achieves a general signification, because the term also revives the custom or disposition to call up ideas of other particular instances and the word becomes associated with each of the things it has customarily been applied to. A particular occurrence of the term 'triangle' thus brings to mind the idea of a particular triangle and revives a custom of calling up other ideas of triangles as needed. It is the fact that a same word has been applied to many resembling individuals that makes such utterances capable of arousing an idea of any other individual sufficiently resembling those individuals. When you hear a word, it cannot call all of these individual things to mind – perhaps only one comes to mind, or a small number (THN 1.1.7.7; SBN 20). Conversing, exchanging sentiments and engaging in social intercourse better acquaints us with general terms and their applications (EPM 5.42; SBN 228).

4.4. SUMMARY

At the beginning of the chapter, we started with a distinction between our 'impressions' and 'ideas' and looked at the connections between them. So far, we learnt that:

■ The origin of ideas is impressions, more specifically, ideas are faint copies of impressions.
■ Ideas may be simple or complex, depending on the simple or complex impressions, which derive from sensation and reflection.
■ Ideas are connected in the faculty of memory and the faculty of imagination.
■ That whatever objects are different are distinguishable, and that whatever objects are distinguishable are separable by the imagination.
■ The imagination works by means of associative principles, namely, resemblance, contiguity and causation, and effects of these principles include relations, substance, and mode.
■ All abstract ideas are particular and these particular ideas used in a certain manner – as representations for a class of things by means of a habit in the imagination with a leaning towards particular resemblances.

Now that the operations of the mind have been explained, Hume turns to apply this mental machinery to a variety of philosophical topics. We begin with space and time.

NOTES

1 Thanks to Martin Coventry and Emma Duncan for help in constructing this diagram. The inspiration for the diagram came from Jim Fieser's entry on Hume's metaphysics and epistemology in the *Internet Encyclopedia of Philosophy*.
2 THN 1.1.1.1; SBN 1; AB 6; SBN 648.

3 See also THN 1.1.1.12; SBN 7; AB 6; SBN 647–8; EHU 2.5; SBN 19.
4 Flew (1986: 21).
5 Bennett (2001: 218–9).
6 Bennett (2001: II, 218).
7 Among those commentators who take the view that the idea of the missing shade can count as complex include Bernard Rollin, 'Hume's Blue Patch and the Mind's Creativity' (1971: 119–8) and John Losee, 'Hume's Demarcation Project' (1992: 51–62).
8 See Stanistreet (2002: 51–2). See also Garrett (1997: 73–4).
9 Stroud (1977: 34).
10 See also Garrett (1997: 50, 55).
11 Stroud (1977: 34).
12 Stroud (1977: 34).
13 Garrett (1997: 52).
14 The discussion in this paragraph is taken from Garrett (1997: 50–2).
15 Garrett (1997: 52).
16 Garrett (1997: 52).
17 Stroud (1977: 34).
18 Bennett (2001: 218).
19 THN 1.1.4.6; SBN 12–3; see also Newton's *Opticks*, especially Query 31.
20 See Hobbes (1994: 12).
21 For a thorough discussion of the seven relations, see Owen (1999: 83 f.).

CHAPTER 5

SPACE AND TIME

Hume's views on the acquisition and connection of ideas, causation, free will, personal identity, scepticism and morals are all unquestionably significant contributions to philosophy, however, his theory about the origin and nature of our ideas of space and time has never been particularly influential.[1] The theory has been judged 'not very attractive',[2] and is generally thought to be the 'least admired'[3] and 'least satisfactory' part of the work, perhaps even 'the least satisfactory in all Hume's publications'.[4] One of the main reasons why scholars find the theory of space and time problematic is that it is thought to represent an exception to the Copy Principle, as there is no simple impression of space or of time.[5] Space and time instead are abstract ideas concerning 'the manner or order in which objects exist' (THN 1.2.4.2; SBN 40).[6]

This chapter surveys Hume's theory about how we arrive at the ideas of space and time and his defense of it.[7] I will then emphasize the importance of his defense of the said theory in relation to other parts of his philosophical project, namely, the theory of truth and his account of causes, morals and aesthetics. In the final section, I turn to interpretive matters in an attempt to show that the account of the origin of the ideas of space and time need not be inconsistent with the first principle.

5.1. AGAINST THE INFINITE DIVISIBILITY OF SPACE AND TIME

One paradoxical notion frequently embraced by philosophers is the doctrine of infinite divisibility, especially that of space and time. Hume is first concerned to debunk this notion before offering his own explanation of how we come by our ideas of space and time.

Hume's arguments against infinite divisibility are based on two universal principles. The first principle states that the capacity of the mind is limited as such a fully adequate conception of infinity, either of the infinitely large or the infinitely small, is not possible (THN 1.2.1.2; SBN 26). Arnauld and Nicole endorsed the principle that the mind is incapable of having any adequate idea of infinity as the finite mind 'gets lost in and dazzled by infinity' (AT 230). That the nature of the limited mind is such that it is unable to understand the infinite is in fact the ninth axiom to be used as one of the 'principles of great truths' (AT 251). Malebranche accepted the principle also; he argued that, 'Anyone who reflects a little on his own thoughts has enough experience to know that the mind. . .cannot penetrate the infinite' (ST 204). Contrary to Hume, Arnauld and Nicole and Malebranche maintain that the finite mind is no impediment to the doctrine of infinite divisibility; Malebranche even uses this principle to defend the infinite divisibility of matter. He argues that 'in order to be convinced of the infinite divisibility of matter, the mind need not understand it' (ST 204; AT 232).

The second principle at the basis of Hume's argument is that 'whatever is capable of being divided infinitely consists of an infinite number of parts'. The idea here is that it is impossible to set the number of parts without setting a boundary or a limit, so no bounds or limits can be set on the number of parts (THN 1.2.1.2; SBN 26–7). Malebranche and Bayle are likely influences here. Malebranche assumes that the infinite divisibility of matter means that objects are composed of an infinite number of parts (ST 26–28) and Bayle reports that 'if matter is divisible to infinity, it actually contains an infinite number of parts' (HD 356).

From these abovementioned two principles,[8] Hume argues that no idea of any finite quantity, any physical object, admits of an infinite division. The mind, due to its finite capacity, always reaches an end in the division of its ideas. By the 'proper distinctions and separations', ideas may be divided into lesser parts which will eventually be 'simple and indivisible' (THN 1.2.1.2; SBN 27). This establishes that the imagination 'reaches a *minimum*', a minimum of ideas incapable of any further subdivision (THN 1.2.1.3; SBN 27). Ideas themselves have a minimum size, where the imagination cannot conceive any further separation. Hume explains by way of the Separability Principle: 'that whatever objects are different are distinguishable, and that whatever objects are distinguishable are separable by the thought and imagination'. We cannot distinguish or separate the idea of a grain of sand into twenty parts, much less one thousand or ten thousand, or an infinite number of parts (THN 1.2.1.3; SBN 27).[9]

Sensory perceptions as well as ideas in the imagination have a minimum size and there is experimental proof that shows this is to be the case (THN 1.2.2.4; SBN 27). Put a spot of ink on a piece of paper. Stare at the spot. Now walk away from the spot without taking your eyes off it until you cannot see it anymore. The moment before the spot vanishes is a simple image or impression or perception that is indivisible. Such an impression is often referred to as a 'minimum visible' or a 'colored point'. Such a minimum visible has no spatial extension, but can be sensed because they are either colored or tangible. The microscope and the telescope supplement the senses but still present a visual field made up of minimal parts (THN 1.2.1.4; SBN 28).

This picture of the nature of reality sketched by Hume is sometimes referred to as *phenomenological atomism* or the doctrine of *minima sensibilia*, the idea that there are indivisible points, or units, or atoms, or corpuscles, or pixels that cluster together in finite arrays to build both our visual and imaginative fields. These minimal points are the ultimate elements from which knowledge of the nature of reality is to be constructed. Hume argues that these minimal ideas in the imagination and minimal sensory impressions, despite some defects, are an adequate representation of the smallest possible parts of any object in the natural world (THN 1.2.2.5; SBN 28). An adequate idea is one that accurately represents an object; particular ideas that adequately represent particular objects reveal the nature of the objects they represent.[10] Hume continues that if, upon the comparison of our ideas to objects, we find that something that '*appears* impossible and contradictory' then we must conclude without hesitation that it 'must be *really* impossible and contradictory' (THN 1.2.2.1; SBN 29). Hume next applies the results of his reasoning to the concepts of space and time to show that what certainly appears to be impossible and contradictory is the doctrine of infinite divisibility of space and time.

To this, Hume sets to establish that the smallest parts of extension and duration cannot be more minute than our most minute ideas of them. He argues that from the repetition of the smallest possible idea of extension itself, itself representing the minutest possible being, the mind can produce a compound idea of extension. The compound idea must be made up of indivisible units or points. An infinite repetition of this idea must result in an infinite extension, so it is contradictory to suppose that a finite extension can contain an infinite number of parts: the inevitable outcome of infinite additions is an infinite, not a finite extension (THN 1.2.2.2; SBN 30).[11] Berkeley makes a somewhat similar point, claiming that 'to say a finite quantity or extension consists of parts infinite in number, is so manifest a contradiction, that everyone at first sight acknowledged it to be so' (PHK §124).[12] In short, the point is that it is contradictory to suppose that finite extension is infinitely divisible is a contradiction: it is to say nothing less than that a finite thing is infinite.

Hume also thinks that it would be a contradiction to suppose that time were composed of an infinite number of parts and uses similar arguments to show that our idea of time is made up of indivisible units or moments (THN 1.2.2.4; SBN 31). It is an 'inseparable' property of time is that each of its parts succeed another and none of them can be co-existent; for that reason the year 1737 cannot concur with the year 1738. Now, if in time we never arrived at an end of the division and if each moment as it succeeds another 'were not perfectly single and indivisible, there wou'd be an infinite number of co-existent moments or parts of time', which is an 'arrant contradiction' (THN 1.2.2.4; SBN 31).

The nature of space and time must conform to our idea of it. Since it is impossible to conceive the infinite divisibility of space and time, it cannot be that our ideas of space and time consist of an infinite number of parts. We can, however, conceive of space and time as being made up of indivisible units. In order to further our understanding of this, Hume applies his first principle, the Copy Principle.

5.2. THE ORIGIN OF OUR IDEAS OF SPACE AND TIME

Every idea is derived from some impression. From what impressions are the ideas of space and time derived? It must be from an impression of sensation, since it is unlikely that space and time derive from our impressions of reflection, which includes our passions, emotions, desires and aversions (THN 1.2.3.3; SBN 33).

The idea of space is obtained from the 'disposition of visible and tangible objects', thereby coming to the mind by two senses: sight and touch (THN 1.2.3.7–15; SBN 35–8). Objects themselves are composed of finite atoms or corpuscles, which are 'endow'd with colour and solidity' (THN 1.2.3.15; SBN 38). The arrangement of the points, their manner of appearing to the senses, is a compound impression consisting of smaller indivisible impressions, the minimally visible points, which represent the idea of extension (THN 1.2.3.4; SBN 34). The arrangement of these colored points is the source of an idea of a particular space. The senses convey to us the impressions of these indivisible points arranged in one way or another. These impressions are then comprehended or conceived by the imagination and it is from the structuring of these impressions that we obtain our idea of space. Space, then, is a manner in which minimum points are ordered or arranged relative to one another.[13]

Since the idea of space is derived from the impressions of indivisible points arranged at intervals from one another, there is no particular impression of space. The idea of space is an abstract idea because it is formed on the basis of an observed resemblance among compound impressions of extended objects, this resemblance covering both impressions of sight and touch and consisting in the arrangement or disposition of points or manner of appearance, in which they all agree (THN 1.2.3.5; SBN 34). Given that all general ideas are particular, it follows that the idea of space in general is nothing more than the idea of a particular space. An experience of impressions of colored points arranged in one manner or another becomes associated with the general term 'space' and in this way made to stand for all possible spaces, just as the idea of a particular triangle or dog can be made to represent all possible perceptions of triangles or dogs. Because of the association of ideas that is set up in the imagination, the term 'space' becomes associated with each of the things it has customarily been applied to. A particular occurrence of the term 'space' thus brings to mind the idea of a particular 'space' and revives a custom of calling up other ideas of space as needed.[14]

Time is given a similar treatment to space. Time is an abstract idea derived from the experience of a group of indivisible moments or 'temporally minimal perceptions',[15] which represent the smallest conceivable moments, appearing in a certain succession or manner. He notes Locke's point that our minds operate at a range of speeds that are 'fix'd by the original nature and constitution of the mind, and beyond which no influence of external objects on the senses is ever able to hasten or retard our thought' (THN 1.2.3.7; SBN 35). The idea of time is a copy of impressions, as they are perceived by the mind at its fixed speed. Since the idea of time is derived from a succession of indivisible perceptions, we cannot conceive of time without experiencing a succession of changeable objects: we need a group of sequential perceptions in order to arrive at the idea of time, 'some *perceivable* succession of changeable objects' (THN 1.2.3.7; SBN 35). While there is no simple impression of time, there are particular experiences of time, a particular succession of minimum perceptions, and from these resembling experiences, we form the general or abstract idea of time (THN 1.2.3.6; SBN 35). Hume argues that both philosophers and the vulgar (the common unphilosophical people) commonly entertain an erroneous notion of time as that which is enduring or unchangeable, that is, time as not involving change or succession. This results from a misunderstanding of the idea of time we really have, by mistaking time for the cause of succession instead of seeing it as the effect of succession (THN 1.2.3.11; SBN 37). Another error Hume identifies concerns those who maintain that a void or vacuum, that is, an empty space in which there is nothing visible or tangible, exists.

5.3. THE VACUUM

The possibility of there being completely empty spaces in the universe, a vacuum, or whether the world is entirely filled with matter, a plenum, was a hotly debated topic in Early Modern philosophy, although concerns about the existence of a vacuum can be traced back to at least Plato (c. 429–347 BCE) and Aristotle. Descartes argued that the notion of a vacuum, that 'in which there is nothing whatsoever', is 'contradictory' (CSM I: 229). His argument for this claim is something like the following: if a body has extension in length, depth and breadth, it warrants the conclusion that it is a substance, as it is a contradiction to suppose that an extension should belong to nothing (CSM I: 230). The same conclusion is then drawn about space, which also is taken to be 'an extension in length, breadth and depth': whatever is extended is an extended substance, so space must be an extended substance (CSM I: 229). An immediate corollary is that there can be no vacuum, for that would require an extended region devoid of body, which is impossible.

It was commonly held that Newton proved that it is 'absolutely necessary that there be a vacuum' for without empty space the motions of the planets and all that follows could be 'inexplicable and impossible' (HD 379). Locke himself had four arguments in favor of the vacuum. First, stretch forth your hand beyond your body. In such a case, you are putting your arm where before there was space without body (ECHU 2.8.20). Second, if God annihilated an object, which we must suppose that he can, then this would create a vacuum (ECHU 2.8.21). Third, the motion of objects ultimately necessitates a vacuum (ECHU 2.8.22), and, finally, we have an idea of the vacuum since we can talk and argue about it (ECHU 2.8.23). This shows that our idea of body is not the same as that of space, for we can think of a space where there is no body. From all of these arguments, Locke concludes that there is a vacuum and that body is not essentially extension (ECHU 2.8.26).

Hume thought that no idea of a vacuum or void is possible. This follows from the fact that the idea of space is nothing but the idea of visible and tangible points distributed in a certain order (THN 1.2.5.1; SBN 53). He considers three objections to his conclusion that there is no such thing as a vacuum. These objections are drawn from various sources such as Locke's *Essay*, Bayle's *Dictionary*, Arnauld and Nicole's *The Art of Thinking* and various Newtonian writers.[16]

The first objection says that disputes about the vacuum have been going on 'for many ages', so we must have an idea of it (THN 1.2.5.2; SBN 54). For how could we possibly argue for so long about something if we really have no idea what we were disputing about?

According to the second objection, the idea of a vacuum can be derived from ideas known to be possible. In the case of the 'two possible ideas of *rest* and *annihilation*', one can conceive that an omnipotent God could annihilate a piece of matter, whilst the other parts remain at rest (THN 1.2.5.3; SBN 54). Now: 'what must we conceive to follow upon the annihilation of all the air and subtile matter in the chamber, supposing the walls to remain the same, without any motion or alteration?' (THN 1.2.5.3; SBN 54). Some answer that if there is nothing, that is, no distance, between the walls then the walls should be touching each other. Descartes gave this response. In the *Principles of Philosophy*, he considers 'what would happen if God were to take away every single body contained in a vessel, without allowing any other body to take the place of what had been removed?' (CSM 1: 231). Descartes' answer is that 'when there is nothing between two bodies they must necessarily touch each other' (CSM 1: 231). The problem with this answer is imagining the walls of the emptied chamber collapsing without moving. If we stick to the ideas of rest and annihilation, the resulting idea is that of the existence of a vacuum, not of walls falling down to touch each other whilst remaining at the same time immoveable.

The final objection is that the idea of a vacuum is unavoidable as it necessary to explain motion. A vacuum is needed because there needs to be empty space 'into which one body must move in order to make way for another' (THN 1.2.5.4; SBN 55). Hume does not want to spend too much time on this third argument because it really lies within the sphere of natural philosophy.

In answering these objections, he warns us that we will be taking things 'pretty deep', beginning with 'the nature and origin of several ideas' (THN 1.2.5.5; SBN 55). First, darkness cannot provide an idea of the vacuum. He argues that the idea of darkness is not a positive idea, 'but merely the negation of light' or 'of colour'd and visible objects' (THN 1.2.5.5; SBN 55). The main point is that the absence or removal of visual or tactile impressions, being a mere negation, cannot give rise to the idea of a vacuum or extension without matter as 'the idea of utter darkness can never be the same as that of vacuum' (THN 1.2.5.5; SBN 56). Similarly, one cannot get an impression of empty space from being suspended in the air, 'softly convey'd along by some invisible power' in an 'invariable motion', even when freely moving one's limbs about back and forth around at the same time (THN 1.2.5.6; SBN 56). Darkness and motion without visual or tactile impressions cannot provide an idea of a vacuum.

What if the idea of a vacuum is produced when darkness and motion are mixed with something visible and tangible? Bodies appear to us separated by distances of varying degrees. Since distance is not the sort of thing that is visible or tangible, it is thought that here is the vacuum or empty space (THN 1.2.5.10; SBN 57). This 'natural and most familiar way of thinking' stands in need of correcting (THN 1.2.5.11; SBN 57). Consider two cases: a person supported in the air freely moving about their limbs without coming into tangible contact with anything and a person who feels something tangible, leaves it, 'and after a motion, of which he is sensible, perceives another tangible object' (THN 1.2.5.13; SBN 58). In both cases, 'the sensation, which arises from the motion' is exactly the same, the only difference between them consists 'merely in the perceiving' of those objects, so if the sensation cannot provide an idea of the vacuum in the first instance, neither can it produce the idea in the second instance (THN 1.2.5.13; SBN 58).

These features help to explain why we can 'falsely imagine' an idea of the vacuum (THN 1.2.5.14; SBN 58). Hume explains three relations between these two types of distance, one 'which conveys the idea of extension, and that other, which is not fill'd with any coloured point' (THN 1.2.5.18; SBN 59), in other words, visible objects separated by an intervals or of the free motion of one's limbs. First, whether we perceive the distance between objects or not, the objects affect the senses in the same manner. Second, 'the second species of distance is found capable of receiving the first' (THN 1.2.5.18; SBN 59). In other words, the unperceivable distance between two objects may be filled with perceivable objects or an 'invisible and intangible distance may be converted into a visible or tangible one, without any change on the distant objects' (THN 1.2.5.16; SBN 59). Third, the two kinds of distance 'have nearly the same effect on every natural phenomenon' and 'all qualities, such as heat, cold, light, attraction, etc., all diminish in proportion to the distance' (THN 1.2.5.17; SBN 59).

The relations between the two types of distance explain 'why we imagine we have an idea of extension without the idea of any object of sight or feeling' (THN 1.2.5.19; SBN 60). A 'general maxim' in the science of human nature is that whenever there is a close relation between two ideas are closely connected, 'the mind is apt to mistake them' (THN 1.2.5.19; SBN 60). Of the three relations between ideas, resemblance, contiguity and cause and effect, resemblance is the most prone to error, although contiguity and cause and effect have the same influence. A case of this is when people 'use words for ideas, and to talk instead of thinking in their reasonings', a mistake made easily by the mind because they are so closely connected (THN 1.2.5.21; SBN 61–2). For the same reason 'we substitute the idea of a distance, which is not consider'd either as visible or tangible, in the room of extension, which is nothing but a composition of visible and tangible points dispos'd in a certain order' (THN 1.2.5.21; SBN 62). Both cause and effect and resemblance are to blame for the mistake: that 'the first species of distance is found to be controvertible to the second' is a kind of cause and 'the similarity of their manner of affecting the senses' develops the relation of resemblance (THN 1.2.5.21; SBN 62).

Hume is now prepared to answer the three objections. First, mere disputes about the vacuum do not 'prove the reality of the idea on which the dispute turns' for people commonly 'deceive themselves in this particular' (THN 1.2.5.22; SBN 62). When it comes to the paradox of the empty chamber whose walls should collapse, Hume supposes that 'when every thing is annihilated in the chamber, and the walls continue immoveable, the chamber must be conceiv'd much in the same manner as present, when the air that fills it is not an object of the senses' (THN 1.2.5.23; SBN 62).

Finally, as for the argument from motion taken from natural philosophy, we know by experience that two bodies separated by an invisible and intangible distance have 'a capacity of receiving body betwixt them, and that there is no obstacle to the conversion of the invisible and intangible distance into one that is visible and tangible' (THN 1.2.5.24; SBN 63). For all we know, motion has the same effect on distant bodies as such a conversion, the 'motion of a body has much the same effect as its creation', this answer at present 'suffices for the imagination' (THN 1.2.5.24; SBN 63). The idea that motion is continuous re-creation comes from Descartes.[17] He argued that the motion in the different parts of the world is 'continually preserved through an action identical with its original act of creation' (CSM I: 42). One importance difference between them is that Descartes thinks God is the one who produces the motion between the parts. Hume, naturally enough, is silent on the issue of whether God is the first cause of the motion in the universe, although it is interesting to note that there is a return to the subject matter in Part 8 of the *Dialogues Concerning Natural Religion*. Here, in his lengthy response to Cleanthes' argument from design, Philo revives an 'old *Epicurean* hypothesis' of an endlessly recurring world, running on pure internal necessity yet with all the appearance of design (DNR 49). Here, Philo supposes that matter might be the origin of motion, without requiring a first mover and argues for the continual conservation of motion throughout eternity, regardless of its ultimate cause.

5.4. THREE OBJECTIONS CONSIDERED

Hume considers three objections to his theory of space and time. The first objection is that such mathematical points are non-entities or nothing and hence cannot make up a real existence such as space. Hume's response is that the objection would be convincing were it not for the fact that these points are not nothing as they possess color or solidity (THN 1.2.4.3; SBN 40).

According to the second objection, if extension consisted of such simple and indivisible points, then these points would always completely penetrate one another the moment that they touched. In response, Hume redefines the notion of penetration. Suppose there are two solid bodies approaching one another. Penetration is 'nothing but the annihilation of one of these bodies, and the preservation of the other, without our being able to distinguish particularly which is preserv'd and which annihilated' (THN 1.2.4.5; SBN 41). With such a definition of penetration, it might be said that upon the union of the two bodies, a 'compounded and divisible' object remains, which may be 'distinguish'd into two parts' (THN 1.2.4.6; SBN 41).

The final objection is that such indivisible points are contrary to many essential features of mathematics (THN 1.2.4.8; SBN 42). Hume's response leads to a long discussion in which he concludes that geometry is an art and not an exact science because it lacks any precise standard of equality (THN 1.3.1.4; SBN 70–1). The concepts of equality and inequality are foundational in geometry (AB 29; SBN 658). When geometers use the notion of equality one thing that could be suggested as to what they are doing are counting infinitely divisible points on a line. This would have the advantage of an exact standard of geometric equality because, in effect, it reduces geometrical equality to arithmetical equality. The disadvantage is that the standard of equality of lines or surfaces based on infinitely divisible quantities is completely ineffective because it cannot be put into practice by the mind. The problem is that the points, whether tangible or visible, which enter into the calculation of any line or surface are so minute, that the finite mind cannot possibly figure out the number: we are never in a position in which we can actually count the points on a line. The upshot is that, 'such a computation will never afford us a standard, by which we may judge of proportions' (THN 1.2.4.19; SBN 45), so that geometry cannot attain to the level of precision required by the doctrine of infinite divisibility (AB 29; SBN 658).

The only other possibility is that we judge equality simply by the general appearance of things, deriving a standard of equality by the comparison of particular objects, thereby rendering 'our imagination and senses the ultimate judges of it' (AB 29; SBN 659). This is actually the only sort of standard of equality proper to geometry. This avoids the problem with the previous possibility: it certainly is useful, since we do use it. These types of comparative judgments are not only 'common', but may also be 'certain' and 'infallible': when presented with the measure of a yard and that of a foot, for example, the mind cannot question that the first is longer than the second (THN 1.2.4.22; SBN 637). Our judgments of this kind are not infallible in every instance however. He notes that we often correct our first judgment after review and reflection as the mind tends to make many mistakes when distinguishing proportions such as greater, less and equal – we pronounce objects to be equal when we first supposed them to be unequal and so on.

This is not the only correction that our judgments undergo: errors are also discovered not only by the juxtaposition of objects, but also by the use of some 'common and invariable measure', which after being successively applied to each, demonstrates their different proportions (THN 1.2.4.23; SBN 47). These corrections may undergo even more corrections depending on the nature of the instruments used in the measuring of bodies, and the amount of care employed in the comparison. Over time, we become accustomed to reviewing, comparing, and correcting our judgments, and the mind naturally supposes 'some imaginary standard of equality, by which appearances and measuring are exactly corrected' (THN 1.2.4.24; SBN 48). So, after correcting many judgments of equality, the imagination, which Hume describes as being 'like a galley put into motion by the oars, carries on its course without any new impulse', proceeds to invent a 'correct and exact standard of that relation', that is 'not liable to the least error or variation' (THN 1.4.2.22; SBN 198). The idea of equality thus is simply that of 'a particular appearance corrected by juxtaposition or a common measure' and the possibility of any correction 'beyond what we have instrument and art to make' is dubbed 'incomprehensible', and a 'mere fiction of the mind' (THN 1.2.4.24; SBN 48).

That the imaginary standard is a natural step for the mind to make after critical reflection is evident in many subjects. In the case of time, the 'various corrections of our measures and their different degrees of exactness' gives us an 'implicit notion of a perfect and entire equality' (THN 1.2.4.24; SBN 48). In the case of the musicians' idea of 'a compleat. . .octave', the appearance of this standard is a natural product of the mind's imaginary powers after engaging in much review and reflection (THN 1.2.4.24; SBN 49). The same is true for the painter with respect to colors, and for the mechanic with respect to motion. Both light and shade and swift and slow are supposed to be capable of an 'exact comparison and equality' (THN 1.2.4.24; SBN 49). Hume lastly discusses lines and curves and how they are distinguished. Here, we correct 'the first appearance by a more accurate consideration' and we do so by means of comparing it with 'some rule', of which we are assured by repeated experiences. After all these comparisons and corrections, the imagination forms the idea of a perfect standard (THN 1.2.4.25; SBN 49).

The introduction of the notion of an imaginary standard in Part 1, Book 2 of the *Treatise* is more important than it might initially seem in Hume's system for the notion of a standard is bound up with his theory of truth.[18] Although truth is explicitly defined twice over in the *Treatise*, it cannot be said that Hume offers an especially detailed account of what he meant by truth and falsity. Indeed, according to W. H. Walsh, Hume's remarks on truth are 'few and unenlightening'.[19] Whatever the case may be there can be no doubt that Hume thought that truth was very important. Pursuing the truth of the matter is a basic human instinct, and he admits that this 'peculiar' love for truth is the 'first source' of his enquiries (THN 2.3.10.1; SBN 448). He certainly believed that there was a 'truth and falsehood in all propositions' concerning his pet subject matter of the science of human nature, and hence 'a truth and falsehood, which lie not beyond the compass of human understanding' (EHU 1.14: SBN 14). Truth is valued because we must exercise our 'genius and capacity' to discover it (whatever is obvious is not valued); truth is also valued to the extent to which the truth discovered is seen to be useful and important to us (THN 2.3.10.4; SBN 449).

There is a problem because many philosophers have spent all their time, lost their money, and even destroyed their health in the pursuit of truth while at the same time, it never appeared that these people had a great interest in the general welfare of humankind. This happens because weaker desires for truth are motivated also by sympathy and by the pleasure that arises from the exercise of a mind engaged in a possibly successful enquiry. In this respect, intellectual pursuits are similar to hunting or gaming. The hunter and gambler suppose that there is some utility in their activities, and winning is a certainly pleasurable upshot of the pursuit, but the hunter and the gambler are not motivated merely by the prospect of such winnings (THN 2.3.10.8–10; SBN 452). Related to this love of knowledge is an implanted curiosity of another kind, and this explains another aspect of our behavior: the penchant for gossip, why some have such an insatiable desire some have to know the 'actions and circumstances' of their neighbors (THN 2.3.10.11; SBN 453).

Hume is typically interpreted as embracing a straightforward correspondence theory of truth,[20] according to which a judgment is true if and only if it corresponds to the facts (there are, of course, many different conceptions of what is meant by correspondence and fact depending on the particular correspondence theory of truth at hand). Truth is first defined in the second book of the *Treatise* in a section entitled, 'Of curiosity, or the love of truth'. Specifically, he defines two types of truth: 'Truth is of two kinds, consisting in the discovery of the proportions of ideas, consider'd as such, or in the conformity of our ideas of objects to their real existence' (THN 2.3.10.2; SBN 448). This two-part definition is repeated in the third book of the *Treatise*, when he famously argues that moral distinctions are not derived from reason: 'Truth or falshood consists in agreement either to the *real* relations of ideas or to the *real* existence and matter of fact' (THN 3.1.1.9; SBN 458). Simply put, Hume thinks that there are truths pertaining to relations of ideas, which include mathematical propositions, and truths pertaining to matters of fact, which includes topics such as morals, politics and natural philosophy. Given that the topic of causation falls under the latter category, truths about causes and effects concern not 'relations of ideas but their real connexions and existence' (THN 2.3.10.11; SBN 453). The important question is: what exactly does Hume mean by agreement with or conformity of our ideas of objects to their 'real existence and matter of fact'?[21]

Hume's essay on aesthetics, 'Of the Standard of Taste', provides a helpful clue in this respect. In the essay he links the phrase 'real existence and matter of fact' with the notion of a 'standard' twice. First, when characterizing the position that it is a waste of time to seek 'real beauty or deformity' because beauty and deformity are qualities that exist in the mind only and not in the object, he equates the expression 'real matter of fact' with a 'standard' (EMPL 230). Second, when discussing how to proceed when evaluating the contradictory judgments of art critics, Hume recommends that we 'acknowledge a true and decisive standard to exist somewhere, to wit, real existence and matter of fact' (EMPL 242). This suggests that a judgment is true if it corresponds to, agrees with, or is in conformity with a 'true and decisive standard' and, that a judgment is false if it conflicts with or diverges from that standard. It would be worthwhile to inquire further into what he means by a 'true and decisive standard'. This issue is taken up in Chapter 7.4, in which Hume's discussion about the standard of equality and his theory of truth are linked to his views about necessary connections, aesthetics and morals.

5.5. SPACE, TIME AND THE COPY PRINCIPLE

Applying the Copy Principle, the Separability Principle and the theory of abstract ideas, Hume has argued that indivisible points or moments constitute the parts of space and time, and that our ideas of space and time are derived from complex impressions of the arrangements of such points. He has also defended his account against objections and explained why we falsely think we have the idea of a vacuum. In defending his theory of space and time, Hume makes some points about the geometrical standard of equality that is related to his theory of truth, not to mention his views about causes, morals and aesthetics, or so I will argue in Chapter 7.

We observed in the Introduction that there is a general dissatisfaction with Hume's account of space and time. One reason for the dissatisfaction is that Hume's account of space and time are thought to be an exception to the Copy Principle. Kemp Smith, for example, reports that the explanation of the idea of space, 'opens with a recapitulation of the principles insisted upon in the introductory sections of the *Treatise*, and it closes with teaching out of keeping with these principles'.[22] There is evidence that perhaps even Hume himself found the discussion unsatisfactory: after devoting Book I, Part 2 of the *Treatise* to space and time, the topic is dropped completely in the *Enquiry*, although some of the arguments concerning infinite divisibility receive an airing in Part 2 of the final section to do with scepticism. The likely reason for the omission is that the account of space and time is related to other parts of his philosophy that are central in the *Treatise*, but whose discussion has been omitted altogether or considerably shortened in the *Enquiry* such as abstract ideas, external objects and the self.[23]

One recent attempt to resolve the puzzle comes from Frasca-Spada in her excellent book, *Space and Self in Hume's Treatise*. She is careful to emphasize the empirical origin of Hume's explanation of space and time,[24] but also admits that the idea of space is 'not easily assimilated into any such simple position as that implied by Hume's principle of the correspondence between impressions and ideas'.[25] While she insists that the Copy Principle is a 'maxim' that is 'not meant to be exceptionless',[26] she claims that 'the farthest the first principle can go concerning matters like the origin of the idea of space is to show that the idea of space is, as it were, a point of singularity in our experience'.[27] In this sense, Frasca-Spada argues, the idea of space and time are different than other ideas 'because they are somehow more directly and specifically related to the self'.[28] So when Hume says that the ideas of space and time are derived from the manner of disposition in which we perceive groups of objects, she treats the manner of disposition as 'an original contribution of the mind to sense-experience'.[29] The immediate problem with this interpretation is that Hume explicitly states that space and time are ideas derived from the manner in which objects affect our senses (THN 1.2.5.26; SBN 64). This would mean, Lorne Falkenstein sensibly pointed out, that the manners of disposition are contributed by experience rather than the mind.[30]

Hume openly admits that there is no simple impression of space or of time, but at the same time, he does not seem to regard his account of the origin of these ideas as inconsistent with the first principle. Not only does he open the discussion with the principle, he writes that to 'discover farther the nature of our ideas of space and time' he will apply the principle that impressions always precede ideas (THN 1.2.3.1; SBN 33), but also ends the discussion some thirty pages later with a resounding commitment to the principle. After defending the non-existence of the vacuum, he acknowledges that few will be satisfied with his account. However, he is perfectly satisfied for his 'intention never was to penetrate into the nature of bodies or explain the secret causes of their operations' (THN 1.2.5.26; SBN 64). In the science of human nature, bodies are known only 'by those external properties which discover themselves to the senses' (THN 1.2.5.26; SBN 64) and he contents himself 'with knowing perfectly the manner in which objects affect my senses, and their connections with each other, as far as experience informs me of them' (THN 1.2.5.26; SBN 64). The ideas of space and time are based on the principles of association in the imagination. This is all we can say about space and time if we base our philosophic conclusions on experience. Moreover, this conception 'suffices' for his philosophy, 'which pretends only to explain the nature and causes of our perceptions, impressions and ideas' and hence suffices for the conduct of life (THN 1.2.5.26; SBN 64). Hume insists on the empirical criterion of impressions and ideas and the relevance of all explanations to human behavior, thereby invoking the first part of his method; the avoidance of exploring the ultimate causes of bodies invokes the fourth.

While there is no simple impression of space or of time *per se*, as space and time are abstract ideas that result from compound sensory impressions, it is no small matter that Hume is careful to trace the origin of each idea to a simple impression in experience. The compound idea of space is made up of simple impressions, and in principle, each indivisible colored point is a distinct sensory impression or perception that cannot be broken down any further.[31] He even shows us how we can experience this simple impression with the experiment of the spot of ink. The fact that we can and must conceive of space as being made up of these indivisible points, coupled with these other considerations, leads Hume to conclude that space is composed of indivisible points. Now the simple impression that is the origin of the idea of space has been found, the next step is to explain how the idea is formed on the basis of the impression, using his theory of abstract ideas. Experience contributes the number of impressions being presented in some order or another and the abstract idea of space is formed from observing resembling groups of indivisible impressions or perceptions appearing in a certain manner or order to the senses. Every idea of space is an idea copied from previous impressions, impressions of 'spatially ordered things'.[32] The idea of space therefore is 'a copy of these colour'd points' in addition to 'the manner of their appearance' (THN 1.2.3.4; SBN 33). Each colored point is a simple impression, capable of being seen or felt but incapable of any further separation by the mind, and each representing the smallest parts of any object.

Each simple indivisible moment that makes up the compound idea of time is also capable of being experienced by the mind.[33] The importance of tracing the idea of time to its originating simple impression is evident when Hume discusses those who commonly entertain an erroneous notion of time as that which is enduring or unchangeable. We can apply the idea of time to unchanging objects by means of a 'fiction':

we may observe, that there is a continual succession of perceptions in our mind; so that the idea of time being for ever present with us; when we consider a stedfast object at five-a-clock, and regard the same at six; we are apt to apply to it that idea in the same manner as if every moment were distinguish'd by a different position, or an alteration of the object. The first and second appearances of the object, being compar'd with the succession of our perceptions, seem equally remov'd as if the object had really chang'd. To which we may add, what experience shews us, that the object was susceptible of such a number of changes betwixt these appearances; as also that the unchangeable or rather fictitious duration has the same effect upon every quality, by encreasing or diminishing it, as that succession, which is obvious to the senses. From these three relations we are apt to confound our ideas, and imagine we can form the idea of a time and duration, without any change or succession (THN 1.2.5.29; SBN 65).

Hume makes clear that we do in fact distinguish out different 'moments' in our perception of unchanging objects. Note the importance of tracing the idea of time to its originating impression. This clarifies what Hume is actually doing. The reason we cannot derive an idea of time or duration from an impression of an unchanging object is that there is nothing in such an impression identifiable as time: there's just an unchanging object. In a changing object, however, we recognize the succession involved in the change, and this is, according to Hume, where we derive the idea of time. We can apply this idea to unchanging objects only by treating the unchanging object as if it had changed, that is, the object in which there is no discernible succession as if it had discernible succession. But there is nothing in the impression that prevents us from attributing succession to it, by a fiction. Now if impressions were genuinely instantaneous, this would not be possible. On Hume's account we cannot have instantaneous impressions. The upshot is that Hume's discussion of the divisibility of time requires us to conclude that there are minimal temporal points. These temporal points are simply the smallest noticeable bits of succession, thus 'the indivisible moments of time must be fill'd with some real object or existence, whose succession forms the duration, and makes it be conceivable by the mind' (THN 1.2.3.17; SBN 39).

Hume's account of the origin of the ideas of space and time need not be inconsistent with the Copy Principle. This is because he finds the simple impression of an indivisible point or moment that is the origin of the idea of space and time. Experiencing a cluster of simple, indivisible perceptions in a certain manner or order helps us to derive the idea of space. Time is another manner in which two or more temporally minimal perceptions or moments are ordered or arranged relative to one another.

NOTES

1 See Alexander Rosenberg's piece on Hume's philosophy of science in Fate Norton (1993: 82).
2 See the editors' Introduction to the Selby-Bigge edition of the *Enquiry* (SBN: xiii).
3 Noxon (1973: 115).
4 Flew (1986: 38).
5 Kemp Smith (1941: 273f.); Fogelin (1985: 34): and Wright (1991: 152).
6 It has even been argued that the abstract ideas of space and time are not even ideas at all. See Waxman (1994: 116–7); he claims that space and time are not 'genuine ideas but mere aspects of perceptions, explicable in terms of natural associative propensities'.
7 My exposition of Hume's very difficult theory of space and time is greatly indebted to Frasca-Spada (1998); Garrett (1997: 53–4); and Newman (1981: 2–3).
8 For a critical assessment of Hume's two principles, see Flew (1986: 39f.).
9 For a thorough discussion of the grain of sand example and its predecessors, see Frasca-Spada (1998: chapter 1).
10 This is related to Locke's definition of adequate ideas, that 'which perfectly represent those Archetypes, which the Mind supposes them taken from' (ECHU 2.31.1).
11 A nice summation of Hume's argument against infinite divisibility is as follows: (1) Whatever is infinite has an infinite number of parts, (2) Whatever has an infinite number of parts is infinitely large, (3) Therefore, nothing finitely extended is infinitely divisible. This argument reconstruction comes from Holden (2002: 5).
12 For further detail regarding the connection between Berkeley and Hume on this matter, see Laird (1932: 68f.).
13 Garrett (1997: 53).
14 Compare to Locke's account of the idea of space (ECHU 2.13.2).
15 Garrett (1997: 53).
16 Frasca-Spada (1998: 161).
17 I am indebted here to the editors' annotation to the Norton and Norton edition of the *Treatise* (2000: 444) for pointing me to the comparison here to Descartes' view of motion in the *Principles of Philosophy*.
18 The ensuing discussion of Hume's theory of truth is taken from my monograph, *Hume's Theory of Causation* (2006: chapter 5).
19 Walsh (1972: 99). I owe thanks to David Owen for pointing me to this article.
20 Walsh (1972: 101); Wright (1983: 20); and Schmitt (1995: 145).

21 Annette Baier suggests that Hume's theory of truth might be something like the prosentential theory of truth: 'to call some claim true is simply to reaffirm it, to agree with it' (1991: 63). This however does not do justice to the correspondence aspect of Hume's definition of truth in which truth and falsehood consists 'in agreement either to the *real* relations of ideas or to the *real* existence and matter of fact' (THN 3.1.1.9; SBN 458).
22 Kemp Smith (1941: 273).
23 This point is well made by Frasca-Spada (1998: 1).
24 Frasca-Spada (1998: 70–4).
25 Frasca-Spada (1998: 64).
26 Frasca-Spada (1998: 157).
27 Frasca-Spada (1998: 75).
28 Frasca-Spada (1998: 75).
29 Frasca-Spada (1998: 75).
30 See Falkenstein's book review on Frasca-Spada's *Space and Self in Hume's Treatise* (1999: 241–9, 244).
31 Frasca-Spada (1998: 157).
32 Garrett (1997: 53–4).
33 I am indebted here in this paragraph to Brandon Watson (2003).

CHAPTER 6

CAUSE AND EFFECT

One of Hume's major aims in both the *Treatise* and the *Enquiry* is to 'explain fully' the relation of cause and effect, and he regards the resulting theory as one of his most important and original contributions to philosophy.[1] His argument to do with reasonings concerning cause and effect, or what has come to be known as his argument about induction, is one of the most famous arguments in the history of philosophy. There remains still today considerable disagreement about what Hume's argument to do with the causal inference amounts to and there are loads of responses to the argument.[2] After outlining the account of the causal inference, in the final section, I consider perhaps the most famous response given to Hume's argument about the causal relation, offered by the great German philosopher Immanuel Kant (1724–1804). It is of course not at all possible to do justice to Kant's very complex theory of causation and the transcendental framework within which it is embedded here; but the importance of Kant's response to Hume warrants a brief assessment of the theory here.[3] The monumental question of whether Kant successfully answered Hume on causality will not be settled by any means;[4] the intention is to merely offer two possible rejoinders to Kant's theory on behalf of Hume.

6.1. THE RELATION OF CAUSE AND EFFECT

As we observed in Chapter 4.4.1, Hume thought that when we imaginatively exercise our understanding, our minds are guided by seven philosophical or 'reasoning' relations which are divided as follows: resemblance, identity, space and time, quantity or number, quality or degree, contrariety, and causes or effects.[5] Hume divides the seven philosophical relations into two classes in the *Treatise*. The first class, including resemblance, contrariety, degree or quality, and quantity or number depend, upon the consideration of related ideas alone and comprises objects of knowledge and certainty. The second class, which includes identity, relations of time and place, and causation, depends on the input of further experience and these are objects of probability (THN 1.3.1.1; SBN 69).

Philosophical relations are produced by comparison 'of those relations either constant or inconstant, which two or more objects bear to each other' (THN 1.3.2.2; SBN 73). Constant relations include resemblance, contrariety, degrees in quality, and proportion in quantity or number. They are called constant because these relations depend entirely on the ideas and change only with a change of its ideas. So, for as long as we do not change our idea of a triangle, a triangle will always have its three angles equal to two right angles. This is an example of proportion in quantity or number. Whether two ideas resemble each other is a function entirely of the ideas themselves. If they are contrary to one another, this can be seen by inspection. We can see from inspection of the ideas of square and circle that no object could be both. Comparisons of the degrees of a quality can also be made on the basis of the ideas themselves. Whether one shade of red is deeper than another is apparent by inspection of the two colors. In each of these cases, the comparison of ideas is made directly, with both ideas fully in view of the mind. Such knowledge is intuitive. We recognize these relations 'at first sight' without the need for any 'enquiry or reasoning' (THN 1.3.1.2; SBN 70). We can also, to some extent, directly compare proportion of quantity and number. That three is greater than two is apparent by comparing the two ideas. The relation of proportion in quantity or number is demonstrative or an example of demonstration. We may have to make a number of comparisons in a chain of ideas. We can be certain regarding each link of the chain, and so can be certain of the whole. In demonstration, it is impossible to conceive of the opposite without implying a contradiction. It is impossible for the addition of two and two to be anything but four and to deny it involves a contradiction.

The inconstant relations include identity, relations of time and place and causation. These are inconstant because they do not depend entirely on the ideas and may be changed with no change in the ideas involved (THN 1.3.1.1; SBN 69). For example, two objects or the ideas of those objects may be left unchanged, yet we can vary or change the distance between those objects. This is an example of the relation of time and place.

Of the seven philosophical relations, three of these relations are also natural relations.[6] Natural relations include the three Principles of the Association of Ideas: resemblance, contiguity, and cause and effect. Note that causation may be either a natural or philosophical relation. Association or the ability of the imagination to unite ideas according to certain principles by a gentle force produces these natural relations. Both resemblance and contiguity in time and place involve two ideas derived from impressions which are both present to the mind. Cause and effect, specifically, are relations of which we receive information from experience and it is the connection of cause and effect which carries us beyond the evidence of our memory and senses. If a person finds a watch on a deserted island, they would conclude automatically that there had once been other humans on the island; if one hears a rational and articulate discourse in complete darkness, they would conclude that other people were present in the room, and so on.[7]

In Section 4 of the *Enquiry*, the topic of relations is dropped in favor of a division of the objects of human reason commonly called 'Hume's Fork': relations of ideas and matters of fact. Relations of ideas have the following features:[8]

- Include everything which is intuitively or demonstrably certain
- Denying them involves a contradiction
- Discoverable by thought alone without evidence of anything existent
- Include pure mathematics (geometry, algebra and arithmetic).

An example is '$3 \times 5 = 15$'. Here we see a logical relation between these ideas that we can be certain of and in fact cannot conceive of as being false. That these relations of ideas are either intuitively or demonstratively certain means that we grasp the certainty of them either immediately, this would be intuition, including resemblance, contrariety, degrees in quality, or through a process of reasoning where it is impossible to conceive the contrary, which is demonstration and includes proportion in quantity and number. This type of relation may be comprehended without any dependence on anything existing in the universe because we understand the truth just by understanding what it says. In many cases, then, the mind is able to gain knowledge merely by examining ideas which it has before its view, as in mathematics. The truth about these relations does not guarantee that statements like '3 ×5 = 15' will always be true. The relations between the ideas will stay exactly the same unless there is a change in the ideas (THN 1.3.1.1; SBN 69).

Matters of facts depend on what experience tells us and have the following features:

- Not intuitively certain
- Denial involves no contradiction
- Involve existence or non-existence of something
- Include everything below the certainty of demonstration.

An example is 'that the sun will rise tomorrow'. This is a matter of fact learnt from experience. Matters of fact are not certain. That is, it is always possible to conceive of the contrary of every matter of fact and it never implies a contradiction if you deny them. 'That the sun will rise tomorrow' is a matter-of-fact statement learnt from experience. It makes perfectly good sense to say that the sun will not rise tomorrow because it is possible to conceive of this state of affairs. The point is that statements of mathematics are certain and independent of experience because they are definitions. For example, it is impossible to conceive or imagine a 'round square' because of the definitions we have assigned to 'round' and 'square'. The definitions which we have assigned to 'sun' and 'rising' make it quite possible to conceive of the sun not rising. Hume is mostly interested in matter of fact statements because they provide us with virtually all of our knowledge of the world (EHU 5.1.2; SBN 41). Matters of facts themselves are based on the relation of cause and effect which in turn are based on experience.

Hume turns to explain this relation of cause and effect; proceeding with the Copy Principle to find out from what impression the idea is derived. Supposing that the idea of causation must be derived from some relation between objects, Hume discovers that objects that stand in the relation of causes and effects are *contiguous*; contiguity is thus deemed essential to causation. The second component to causes and effects is *priority in time* – the cause must be temporally prior to the effect.[9] Another essential relation to causation is *constant conjunction*. Through experience, we learn that certain events have always been attended with certain effects, that heat has always attended flame for example and we call one 'cause' and the other 'effect'. The most important element to causation is that of a necessary connection (THN 1.3.2.11; SBN 77). In fact, in the *Enquiry*, Hume challenges one to 'define a cause, without comprehending, as a part of the definition, a *necessary connection* with its effect' (EHU 8.25; SBN 95). In sum, this means that when A causes B, if A occurs, then B *must* occur: B absolutely must follow on the occurrence of A. For A to be the cause of B, then not only must A and B be spatio-temporally contiguous, and not only must A precede B; but A and B must also be necessarily connected.

Before he can discuss what constitutes a necessary connection or how it is to be defined, Hume says that he must answer two other questions:

(1) 'For what reason we pronounce it *necessary*, that every thing whose existence has a beginning, shou'd also have a cause?'
(2) 'Why we conclude, that such particular causes must *necessarily* have such particular effects; and what is the nature of that *inference* we draw from the one to the other and of the *belief* we repose in it?' (THN 1.3.2.14–5; SBN 78).

Each question is taken in turn.

6.2. WHY A CAUSE IS ALWAYS NECESSARY

It is generally thought that the maxim in philosophy that 'whatever begins to exist, must have a cause of existence' is intuitively or demonstratively certain. This was thought to be so by Hobbes[10] and Locke (ECHU 4.10.3), amongst others. Hume denies that this maxim is intuitively or demonstratively certain. First, the maxim is not an example of the constant relations, in other words, the maxim does not turn of any of the four relations, resemblance, quantity or number, degree or quality, and contrariety. His main argument has to do with the imagination's ability to separate ideas wherever it can perceive a difference between them, that is, the Separability Principle, coupled with the maxim borrowed from Descartes that 'nothing we imagine is absolutely impossible' (THN 1.2.2.8; SBN 32). From these two principles, Hume draws the consequence that the cause and the beginning of existence are not the same thing. This is because we can imagine one without imagining the other. If so, then these two principles require us to hold that a beginning of existence without a cause is not impossible. In sum:

(1) All distinct ideas are separable.
(2) The ideas of cause and effect are separable; the idea of a cause of existence is distinct from the idea of a beginning of existence.
(3) We can conceive of something beginning to exist without a cause.

Since it is possible for the mind to conceive of an object to be non-existent one moment and existent the next, it is possible to conceive of something existing without a cause. If the maxim that whatever begins to exist must have a cause of existence were intuitively or demonstratively true, then we could not have the conception. This follows from the fact that to be intuitive or demonstrative means that the opposite cannot be conceived. We can conceive the opposite. Therefore, the maxim is neither intuitive nor demonstrative (THN 1.3.3.3; SBN 79–80).

Since the principle is not demonstrative, it follows that any purported rational justification of the principle that every beginning of existence has a cause will be fallacious. Hume briefly considers Hobbes, Clarke and Locke's efforts to demonstrate the necessity of a cause for any given effect. Hobbes claims that unless there was a cause nothing could begin to exist; everything would remain in 'eternal' suspense (THN 1.3.3.4; SBN 80). Hume argues that this assumes what is to be proven, namely, that everything has a cause for its existence. Hobbes' argument begs the question. Clarke argues that if anything lacked a cause it would produce itself and therefore must have existed before itself. This is impossible, so everything must have a cause for its existence. Hume thinks this also begs the question, Clarke assumes what he is trying to prove. Hume also argues that there is a difference between not having a cause and being one's own cause. Locke's demonstration also begs the question. Locke argued that if something is produced by no cause, then it must be produced by nothing. Nothing can never be a cause. Therefore, everything has a cause of its existence. Like the other arguments, this is based on the assumption that everything must have a cause. This is the assumption is what Hume is challenging. We cannot prove something by assuming it, for if we did then we would prove anything we wanted to.[11]

It is worth emphasizing that while Hume denies that the maxim is intuitively or demonstratively certain, he certainly does not question the truth of the maxim.[12] He accepts the causal principle, for instance, in his discussion of liberty and necessity in the *Enquiry*, stating that, 'it is universally allowed that nothing exists without a cause of its existence' (EHU 8.25; SBN 95) and he goes on to argue that it is compatible with liberty. Further evidence is the 1754 letter to John Stewart in which he declares: 'I never asserted so absurd a Proposition as *that any thing might arise without a cause*: I only maintain'd, that our Certainty of the Falshood of that Proposition proceeded neither from Intuition nor Demonstration; but from another Source'.[13] The source is experience. Exactly how does experience give rise to such a principle? He 'sinks' this question into another question: '*Why we conclude, that such particular causes must necessarily have such particular effect, and why we form an inference from one to another?*' (THN 1.3.3.9; SBN 82).

6.3. THE INFERENCE FROM CAUSE TO EFFECT

In causal reasoning, the mind goes beyond the present objects of perception and infers the existence of either a cause or an effect which is not immediately present to perception. Nevertheless, there must be some impressions or an idea of memory, which by definition is almost as vivid as an impression, be immediately present in perception. If not, then our entire reasoning would be without a foundation. Instead of carrying on our inferences *ad infinitum*, a present impression provides a foundation which removes doubt and the necessity for further inquiry. For example, we believe that Caesar was killed 'in the senate-house on the *ides* of *March*' because we have read about the killing in history books and we suppose that 'this fact is establish'd on the unanimous testimony of historians, who agree to assign this precise time and place to that event' (THN 1.3.4.2; SBN 83). Historians obtain their information from reports, letters, documents, and so on. These reports are the results of original testimony of eyewitnesses and spectators. Eventually, we must find the impression which serves as the ultimate foundation for the inference.

There are three stages in a cause and effect inference:

(1) There is an original impression.
(2) There is a transition to an idea of the connected cause or effect.

(3) There is a special quality attached to the inferred idea, namely, belief or assent (THN 1.3.5.1; SBN 84).

The question of where the original impression comes from is irrelevant to the present discussion. We don't know the ultimate causes of our impressions of the senses. If the original impression comes from external physical objects, from God, or from our own mind, it does not matter. Our perceptions have enough coherence to form a self-contained system.

Memory supplies us with ideas almost as vivid as impressions and we base further inferences on the trust we place in our memory. The first part of the causal inference involves the immediate presence of an impression or vivid idea of memory; from this we infer an idea. The idea is contiguous to and successive of the first impression or vivid idea. Moreover, it is because the second or inferred idea was constantly conjoined in past experience with the first impression or vivid idea of memory that we infer the second from the first. The causal inference depends on contiguity, succession and constant conjunction. On this basis, we suppose that other objects which are similar in appearance will be attended with similar effects, and infer the existence of the one from that of the other (THN 1.3.6.2–3; SBN 87; AB 9; SBN 649).

Hume's next move concerns whether experience produces the inference by reason or an association in the imagination. If it were reason, it would proceed on the 'uniformity principle': '*That instances, of which we have had no experience, must resemble those, of which we have had experience, and the course of nature continues always uniformly the same*' (THN 1.3.6.4; SBN 89; AB 13; SBN 651). The idea is that we expect like effects to those we have experienced will follow from them. If someone hands us something like bread we have eaten in the past, we will repeat the experiment without thinking about it and foresee with certainty that it will indeed nourish us like before. Hume wants to know the foundation of that inference. Why do I suppose that the bread that nourished me today will continue to do so in the future? The inference under question is the following:

(a) I have found that such an object has always been attended with such an effect.
(b) Therefore, other objects which are similar in appearance will be attended with similar effects (EHU 4.2.16; SBN 34).

Hume thinks this is a 'just' inference, and it is an inference we use all the time in daily affairs. However, (b) is not a necessary consequence of (a). There is an extra step or an inference that the mind needs to make in order to make the inference from (a) to (b) (EHU 4.2.16; SBN 34).

That the causal inference is founded on reason is rejected with the following argument. If the inference is founded on reason, then the Uniformity Principle must be founded on either demonstrative or probable reasoning as there are only two types of reasoning: demonstrative reasoning concerning relations of ideas and probable reasoning concerning matters or fact. Demonstrative reasoning cannot found the principle because it is always possible to conceive a change in the course of nature and this 'sufficiently proves' that such a change is not impossible (THN 1.3.6.5; SBN 89; EHU 4.2.18; SBN 35). All demonstrations are certain and imply the impossibility of conceiving a contrary case. It is easy to conceive or imagine a change in the course of nature so that the future will not resemble the past. Since we can conceive of the future being different from the past, we cannot be certain about it. There is no contradiction in supposing the course of nature may change and that causes like those we have previously experienced, may be attended with different effects. It is perfectly conceivable for instance: 'that a body, falling from the clouds, and which, in all other respects, resembles snow, has yet the taste of salt or feeling of fire' (EHU 4.2.18; SBN 35).

Probable reasoning cannot found the Uniformity Principle either, because probable reasoning is based on the supposition that the future must conform to the past and therefore can never prove it, because 'the same principle cannot be both the cause and the effect of another' (THN 1.3.6.7; SBN 90; AB 14; SBN 651). This move is circular reasoning: we would be assuming what we are supposed to be proving, hence 'taking for granted the very point in question' (EHU 4.2.19; SBN 36). Since the uniformity principle cannot be founded on either demonstrative or probable reasoning, reasoning 'fails us in the discovery of the ultimate connexion of causes and effects' (THN 1.3.6.11; SBN 91). Consequently, 'even after we have experience of the operations of cause and effect, our conclusions from that experience are *not* founded on reasoning or any process of the understanding' (EHU 4.2.15; SBN 32). It might be said that, 'from a number of uniform experiments, we infer a connexion between sensible qualities and the secret powers,' but Hume argues that this is the same difficulty couched in different terms and runs the same argument against it (EHU 4.2.21; SBN 36–7; THN 1.3.6.10; SBN 90).

One might object that his practice refutes his doubts (EHU 4.2.21; SBN 38). Hume's response is that it mistakes the question, as an agent, he is satisfied with the inference, but as a philosopher, he wants to learn the foundation of the inference. He is clear that he has great trust in past experience, nonetheless, he has a philosophical curiosity to investigate the foundation of our trust. He confesses at present he has no idea 'and if I be wrong, I must acknowledge myself to be indeed a very backward scholar; since I cannot now discover an argument, which. . .was perfectly familiar to me, long before I was out of the cradle' (EHU 4.2.23; SBN 39).

Although reasonings from cause and effect are not founded on reason, Hume assures us that there is 'no danger that these reasonings, on which almost all knowledge depends, will be affected by this discovery' (EHU 5.1.2; SBN 41). He argues that the mind is induced to make this inference by a principle of nature with an 'equal weight and authority', custom or habit, a universally acknowledged principle of human nature. Customary associations are based on the repeated experience of cause-effect relations. After such experience, the person expects the effect. From the experience of constant conjunction between causes and effects, the objects acquire a union in the imagination, and when the impression of one strikes us, we 'immediately form an idea of its usual attendant'; it is because of this custom, that the mind passes naturally from the idea of flame to the idea of heat (THN 1.3.7.15; SBN 93). The imagination unites the ideas of cause and effect as a natural relation. Thus, it is only as a natural relation that cause and effect inferences are believed and that the inference is assented to. The association of ideas then is an essential part of reasoning concerning cause and effect, the ultimate principle on which we base all our conclusions on experience. Custom is the great guide of human life, for without it life would be more or less impossible, 'We should never know how to adjust means to ends. . .There would be an end at once of all action' (EHU 5.1.6; SBN 44–5; AB 16; SBN 652).

He does not pretend to explain why custom or habit produces the propensity to extend the past into the future. He simply points out that this is an ultimate principle which is universally acknowledged. At this point, we can stop our philosophical researches: we cannot advance a single step farther. We have reached an operation of the mind that is essential to the subsistence of all human creatures. Confirmation of this theory is that custom is the great guide of animal life too.

6.3.1. The reason of animals

Animals learn from experience and infer that the same events always follow from the same causes based on custom (THN 1.3.16.6–7; SBN 178). It is 'instinct. . .which teaches a man to avoid the fire, as much as that, which teaches a bird. . .the art of incubation, and the whole economy and order of its nursery' (EHU 9.6; SBN §85). As an example of how animals reason, Hume points to the 'ignorance and inexperience of the young' in contrast to the cunning and wisdom of old animals who have learnt from long observation to avoid what hurts them and to pursue what gives them ease or pleasure (EHU 9.2; SBN 105). Dogs know to avoid fire and know when their masters are angry just from the tone of voice. These are all conjectures founded on experience. This is still more evident from the effects of discipline and education on animals so that they may be taught a course of action contrary to their natural instincts and propensities (EHU 9.3; SBN 105). Hume thinks that it is impossible that this inference of the animal, by which like effects are expected from like causes, is the effect of reasoning (EHU 9.5; SBN 106). It is custom alone which guides animals in making this inference. Such learning is instinctual and habit-based in animals and probably it is similarly based in us. The habit of reasoning in both humans and animals is one of the implanted principles of nature and is thus able to influence us.

There are differences between human and animal reasoning however. Humans far surpass animals in their reasoning; just as there are great differences amongst humans when it comes to reasoning ability. These include differences in memory and attention, the ability to detach oneself and overcome one's own biases and emotions, and inferential ability. Some people are better at carrying on a 'chain of consequences to a greater length than another', others are better at seeing the 'bigger picture' so to speak while others are able to think for longer without running into confusion and so on (EHU 9.5n20; SBN 107n). Those who think with haste or with a narrowness of mind which sees not all sides are considered will be prone to commit mistakes in causal reasoning. Also, those who have 'acquired a confidence in human testimony, books and conversation enlarge much more the sphere of one man's experience and thought than those of another' (EHU 9.5n20; SBN 107n). Animals thus have thought and knowledge of matters of fact like ours in kind, although to a lesser extent. Humans have more self-awareness about the learning process; a better grasp of complications, the ability to chain together longer inferences and formation of explicit generalizations and greater information access thanks to the ability to converse through language: we can learn from others' experiences via their testimony, not to mention access to books. The reason of animals will be important in the theory of the passions in Book 2.

6.4. BELIEF

Having explained the formation of the inference from cause to effect, Hume now turns specifically to the third part of the second question raised about causation: What about the nature of the *belief* we repose in the causal inference? Hume emphasizes often that it is a difficult topic to write about, and he famously expresses dissatisfaction with his doctrine of belief in the Appendix to the *Treatise*, admitting that he is at a 'loss for terms to express [his] meaning' (THN 1.3.7.7; SBN 628). Nevertheless, this is a very important topic for Hume to investigate because when reasoning from causation, the imagination has complete control over all its ideas and is free to conceive the contrary, even if we do not believe it.[14] For example, although I am able to conceive that the sun will not rise tomorrow, I nevertheless *believe* that the sun will rise tomorrow and act accordingly, by making plans for the next day, setting my alarm clock and so on. What needs to be explained is the difference between actually believing a proposition and merely conceiving it in the imagination. Hume thought new territory was being uncovered here, a new philosophical issue: 'What then is this belief?' and how it differs from mere conception 'is a new question unthought of by philosophers' (AB 17; SBN 652; THN 1.3.7.5n; SBN 97n).

One possibility is that belief adds something new, some new idea, to what is being conceived.[15] He rejects this possibility insisting that belief adds nothing new to what is already conceived. Hume's argument that belief does not involve a separate idea concerns some claims about existence. He argues every idea carries existence with it: to conceive of something and to conceive of it as existing are one and the same operation, so there is no separate idea of existence that could be annexed to another idea to make it a belief. Consider believing in the existence of God and merely conceiving of God. The idea of God and the idea of God existing must be the very same idea, otherwise it would not be possible to distinguish between believing in, on the one hand, and merely conceiving of, on the other hand, the very same thing. If the difference involved a change in what was conceived, thereby understanding existence as a separate idea to which we join to the idea of his other qualities and can again separate and distinguish from them, then we would not have the same thing now conceived, and then believed. This is because any alteration to an idea changes the idea into an idea of something else. The belief of existence brings no new idea to those which compose the idea of the object, 'When I think of God, when I think of him as existent, and when I believe him to be existent, my idea of him neither encreases nor diminishes' (THN 1.3.7.2; SBN 94). Note that the idea remains the same both as merely conceived and as believed.

Since belief is not a matter of annexing a separate idea of existence to the idea of any object conceived, the difference between belief and mere conception must lie in the manner of conceiving. Belief adds nothing new and changes only the manner of conception: a believed idea must be conceived of in a different manner, a belief *feels* different: 'when we are convinc'd of any matter of fact, we do nothing but conceive it, along with a certain feeling, different than what attends the mere reveries of the imagination' (THN 1.3.7.7; SBN 624). Feeling or sentiment thus distinguishes belief from mere conception and such belief differs than mere conception even though the content of an idea believed is no different from that of the same idea merely conceived.

Entering into this operation of the mind called belief is a present impression, a lively idea and an association in the imagination between the impression and idea. We have a present idea or impression. Custom then carries us to conceive of the object which usually accompanies the first idea or impression. The inferred idea is accompanied by a feeling or sentiment of belief, so we believe in the existence of the object represented by the associated idea that has been brought to mind. An inferred idea is believed if it is almost as vivid as the first impression or vivid idea of memory, which is the foundation and first stage of the causal inference. Belief hence is 'nothing but a more vivid, lively, forcible, firm, steady conception of an object' (EHU 5.2.12; SBN 49–50). A believed idea feels more vivid because vivacity has been transferred from the first lively idea or present impression to the inferred idea, hence the definition of belief as 'a lively idea related to or associated with a present impression' (THN 1.3.7.5; SBN 96).[16] The operation of the mind called belief goes on without us noticing as in the case of a person who stops short of crossing a river. Based on past experience, the person 'foresees the consequences of his proceeding forward', but surely does not stop to reflect on past experiences, instead, the mind makes the transition immediately, 'the custom operates before we have time for reflection' (THN 1.3.8.13; SBN 103–4). Belief then is a form of habit as it arises immediately without any operation of the understanding, and he calls anything custom, 'which proceeds from a past repetition, without any new reasoning or conclusion' (THN 1.3.8.10–13; SBN 102–3; EHU 5.5; SBN 43).

That the difference between belief and fiction is one of feeling or sentiment is proved by experience.[17] Consider the difference between reading a fine history of an actual war, by contrast to a fictional recounting of a war. Reading the true history gives one a very different feeling about the events portrayed than it does reading a fictional narrative of imagined events. Belief consists in an idea accompanied by this feeling about the reality of the events, a feeling very different from the feelings that accompany imaginary or fictional creations.

Given that belief is an act of the more sensitive part of our natures, Hume concludes that:

> All probable reasoning is nothing but a species of sensation. 'Tis not solely poetry and music, we must follow our taste and sentiment, but likewise in philosophy. When I give preference to one set of arguments above another, I do nothing but decide from my feeling concerning the superiority of their influence (THN 1.3.8.12; SBN 103).

Hume is not saying here that human beings are completely subjective and irrational. He means that the same principles in the imagination explain all the moral sciences: logic, morals, criticism and so on. He is reaffirming his conviction that the science of human nature based on the experimental method is applicable in all the sciences.

6.4.1. The causes of belief

A general maxim in the science of human nature is that a present impression *'not only transports the mind to such ideas as are related to it, but likewise communicates to them a share of its force and vivacity'* (THN 1.3.8.2; SBN 98). By way of illustration, Hume explains how all the ways in which ideas are associated create the feeling of belief, offering three experiments which show that belief depends on past regularity, custom and the communication of vivacity. The examples of resemblance, contiguity, and causation show that a present impression combined with a relation in the imagination may enliven an idea and produce belief or assent. Upon the appearance of the picture of an absent friend, our idea of the friend and related passions is made more vivid and is enlivened by the resemblance, and 'every passion which the idea occasions, either joy or sorrow, acquires a new force and vigor' (THN 1.3.8.3; SBN 99; EHU 5.2.15; SBN 51). If the picture bears no resemblance, it does not convey a thought of him or her at all; and where it is absent, as well as the person, the idea is weakened.

In the case of contiguity, distance diminishes the force of every idea. So for example being in the vicinity of home makes for more vivid ideas than being very distant: 'When I am a few miles from home, whatever relates to it touches me more nearly than when I am two hundred leagues distant' (THN 1.3.8.5; SBN 100; EHU 5.2.17; SBN 52).

Causation also has the same effect. Some people like the relics of saints and holy people 'in order to inliven their devotion, and give them a more intimate and strong conception of those exemplary lives, which they desire to imitate' (THN 1.3.8.6; SBN 101; EHU 5.2.19; SBN 53). In short, owning the possessions of saints shortens the causal route to them. In all three cases, 'the belief of the correlative object is always presupposed', otherwise the relation would not have an effect. For example, contiguity to home can never enliven our ideas unless we really believe that it exists (EHU 5.2.20; SBN 53).

Hume maintains that the relations of contiguity and resemblance have an inferior effect on the imagination to those of causation, but he believes that they can augment or assist the relation of cause and effect 'with more force in the imagination' (THN 1.3.9.5; SBN 109). In the case of contiguity, pilgrims who have been to the Holy Land are more zealous believers. In the case of resemblance, Hume poses the case of communication of motion by impulse. That this occurs cannot be proved, since we can conceive of many 'consistent and natural' different outcomes (THN 1.3.9.10; SBN 111). So why do we expect motion upon impulse? Because the effect resembles the cause: 'Resemblance, then, has the same or a parallel influence with experience; and as the only immediate effect of experience is to associate our ideas together, it follows, that all belief arises from the association of ideas' (THN 1.3.9.10; SBN 112). Credulity or 'too easy faith in the testimony of others' is also best explained by resemblance (THN 1.3.9.12; SBN 112). Experience teaches us the principles of human nature from which we gather the veracity of human testimony as well as other things. Yet we seldom regulate ourselves by it, believing in all kinds of prodigious events such as 'apparitions, enchantments, and prodigies' (THN 1.3.9.12; SBN 112). This is explained by alleged resemblance between the ideas people have and the facts which they report.

On the other hand, there is a lot of real incredulity among the vulgar about a future state. By this, Hume means a widespread indifference about how one will spend eternity, assuming there is an afterlife, whereas people are quite concerned about what will happen on earth, to their name, to their family, friends and country after they die. The reason for the indifference is that the future state bears so little resemblance to our current state. There is a lack of resemblance between the experiences of this life and the projections made regarding the forms of life after death. An example is the way Catholics condemn massacres, even while believing that the infidel will burn in hell, 'All we say in excuse for this inconsistency is that they really do not believe what they affirm concerning a future state' (THN 1.3.9.14; SBN 115). We also enjoy being scared when it comes to stories of terror from the pulpit and dramatic performances, but we cannot stand fear and terror in real situations (THN 1.3.9.15; SBN 115).

Education is a second kind of custom. Frequent repetition fixes ideas in the imagination and this sort of process can have the same effect as constant conjunction. Custom has such a strong influence as seen in the effects produced by tradition, religious ceremonies and education that it can cause us to believe things that are contrary to experience, just as liars by the frequent repetition of their lies come at last to believe their own lies (THN 1.3.9.19; SBN 117). Many other instances are given, servants feeling the presence of the dead master, people who become familiar with someone just by hearing about them (THN 1.3.9.18; SBN 117). With a touch of irony, he points out that other philosophers will reject his theory because of their own education (THN 1.3.10.1; SBN 118).

6.4.2. The influence of belief

The belief sentiment has a great influence on our passions and imagination and is the governing principle of all of our decisions and actions. The chief springs and moving principles of human action are pleasure and pain. Pleasure and pain may appear as either impressions or ideas. The influence of these on our actions is 'far from being equal', '[i]mpressions always actuate the soul. . .in the highest degree' (THN 1.3.10.2; SBN 118). Belief can make 'an idea approach an impression in force and vivacity' and this allows ideas to have an influence equal to impressions in terms of 'actuating the will' (THN 1.3.10.3; SBN 119). The influence of belief thus is very important in the realm of human action or behavior. Probable reason or belief influences action. Belief depends on custom. Therefore, action depends on custom. Hume expands on this in Book 2 of the *Treatise*, 'Of the Passions'.

6.5. PROBABILITY

Hume divided human reasoning into two types: demonstrative and probable. Within the class of probable reasoning, there is a further distinction between proof and probability.[18] The difference between proof and probability concerns the degree of assurance they offer, proofs affording a superior kind of evidence. Specifically, proofs are arguments based on the relation of cause and effect that are completely free from doubt or opposition because experience teaches that the connexion between the cause and the effect is invariable, for example: 'that the sun will rise tomorrow', 'that all human beings must die' (EHU 6.4; SBN 57). Probabilities are arguments from experience that produce a lower degree of assurance. This is because the evidence is still attended with uncertainty, that is, the connection between causes and effects has so far found to be irregular. For example: 'rhubarb has not always proved a purge, and opium has not always proved a soporific to every one, who has taken these medicines' (EHU 6.4; SBN 57–8). Linguistic concerns prompt the distinction. In common discourse we assume many arguments based on cause and effect that exceed probability, for example, that the sun will rise tomorrow or that the all human beings must die. A person would appear mad if they asserted in everyday conversation that it was only probable that the sun will rise tomorrow, or that all human beings must die.[19]

Arguments are probable or uncertain in two ways: when founded on chance or when founded on causes. Chance is nothing but the ignorance of causes or more properly, the 'negation' of cause or a total indifference or absence of determination in thought (THN 1.3.11.4–5; SBN 125). He notes that where there are no limits on chances, everything becomes equally possible. Where there is no degree of past regularity, there is no opportunity for a habit of the mind to develop. When we do not know the cause, we are indifferent, so that all chances are equal. When we do reason about probability, we find that there is a combination of chances and causes. Some events are not certain, but they do occur with a certain degree of regularity. A superior number of chances produces a superior degree of belief, and the vivacity of the believed idea is proportionate to the degree of probability. For example, if our die has six sides but if two of the sides have the same number, then our belief increases that the number which is repeated will face up more often. If three sides have the same number, then our belief is even greater.

There are three sorts of probabilities to do with causes. The first is due to not enough cases, the second to contrary cases, the third to cases that are not perfectly resembling. In each sort, the probabilities of causes are derived from association of ideas with present impressions. He contends that the strength of customs and habits vary in terms of the constancy of the conjunctions. In making probable judgments, we assume that the future will resemble the past, an assumption based upon habit. And we expect past irregularities and regularities to occur in the future with the same degree of irregularity and regularity respectively. The same principle of extending proportion in the past to proportion in the future is found in the operation of our passions. Experience of constant conjunction, contrary causes, and analogy all rely upon invigoration of the imagination, here resemblance and constant conjunction convey force and vivacity of impressions to related ideas, which we are said to assent to or believe.

All kinds of probability discussed so far are 'reasonable foundations of belief and opinion' (THN 1.3.13.1; SBN 143). There are, however, four types of 'unphilosophical probability', which are *not* reasonable grounds of belief or opinion. The first concerns the fact that beliefs vary with the circumstance, particularly the variations in vivacity that may result from the temporal distance of the experiments: 'The argument, by which we found on any matter of fact we remember, is more or less convincing, according as the fact is recent and remote' (THN 1.3.13.1; SBN 143). The second is that experiments which are recent in memory have a superior influence on our judgment and passions. For example: 'a drunkard who has seen his companion die of a debauch, is struck with that instance for some time, and dreads a like accident for himself: But as the memory of it decays away. . .his former security returns' (THN 1.3.13.2; SBN 144). The third concerns variations of vivacity that result from the length of arguments, 'a man may receive a more lively conviction from a probable reasoning, which is close and immediate, that from a long chain of consequences, tho' just and conclusive in each part' THN 1.3.13.3; SBN 144).

The final type of unphilosophical probability has to do with hastily formed '*general rules*' which are the source of prejudices such as 'An *Irishman* cannot have wit, and *Frenchman* cannot have solidity; for which reason, tho' the conversation of the former in any instance be visibly very agreeable, and of the latter very judicious' (THN 1.3.13.7; SBN 146–7). Such general rules are formed from habit. Thus, while custom is the foundation of all judgments, sometimes it has an effect on the imagination in opposition to the judgment. These sorts of propensities of the imagination can be corrected by reflecting on a more stable kind of general rules, like the rules to judge causes and effects.

6.6. RULES TO JUDGE CAUSES AND EFFECTS

Hume offers eight general rules to help us regulate our judgments concerning causes and effects; these rules are supposed to help us determine when objects really do lie in the relation of cause and effect. Our judgments are based on custom, but we do need to make sure that we supplement, and correct our custom by self-conscious reasoning. When we review a rashly formed general rule, a prejudice for instance, and compare it with 'more general and authentic operations of the understanding', we find it to be of an 'irregular nature', and thus reject it (THN 1.3.13.12; SBN 150). The rules themselves are 'formed on the nature of our understanding and on our experience of its operations in the judgments we form concerning objects' – that is, the rules are formed by reflecting on our cognitive mechanisms and observing our own successes and failures of their past employment in causal reasoning (THN 1.3.13.11; SBN 149).[20]

The function of the rules, therefore, is to correct errors in causal reasoning, which frequently arise because the causes are very complicated in their operations. For, in the production of almost any effect, there is a complication of circumstances, some of which are essential to the effect, and some of which, although frequently conjoined with the essential circumstances, are superfluous. The superfluous factors, however, may still have an effect on the imagination. For example, suppose that c is known to be sufficient and necessary for the production for e. However, when c produces e, it is conjoined with d, which is entirely incidental to the production of e. The effect of the conjunction of d with c is that the imagination extends the principle c causes e to the resembling circumstance c and d causes e. The imagination can even be led to expect production of e when d is present and c is absent. If we are to reason correctly about causal relationships, however, it is necessary that we correct this propensity of the imagination and not include accidental circumstances in the description of causal relations.[21] Thus by reflecting on the rules, 'we learn to distinguish the accidental circumstances from the efficacious causes' (THN 1.3.13.11; SBN 149).

Hume's first rule states that causes and effects must be contiguous in space and time; the second rule states that the cause must be before the effect; and the third rule states that there must be a constant union betwixt the cause and effect. The fourth rule, which states that, 'The same cause always produces the same effect, and the same effect never arises but from the same cause', is the source of 'most of our philosophical reasonings' (THN 1.3.15.6; SBN 173). This rule is clearly inspired by Newton's second rule, which states that 'to the same natural effects, we must, as far as possible, assign the same causes' (MP II: 398). In fact, in the *Enquiry Concerning the Principles of Morals*, Hume calls rule four 'Newton's chief rule of philosophizing' (EPM 3.2.48; SBN 204). Rules five and six both depend on the fourth rule. The former states that: 'where several different objects produce the same effect, it must be by means of some quality, which we discover to be common amongst them' and according to the latter: 'The difference in the effects of two resembling objects must proceed from that particular, in which they differ' (THN 1.3.15.8; SBN 174).

The seventh rule states that, 'The absence or presence of one part of the cause is supposed to always be attended with the absence or presence of a proportional part of the effect' (THN 1.3.15.9; SBN 174). He cautions, however, that in this case we ought to 'beware not to draw. . .a conclusion from a few experiments'. For instance a certain degree of heat gives pleasure, if you diminish the heat, the pleasure diminishes, but it does not follow that if you continue to augment it that the pleasure will likewise augment; instead we find it to degenerate into pain. The last rule states that 'an object, which exists for any time in its full perfection without any effect, is not the sole cause of the effect but requires to be assisted by some other principle, which may forward its influence and operation' (THN 1.3.15.10; SBN 174). This final rule has already made an appearance in establishing priority in time as one of the four essential components of causes and effects (THN 1.3.2.7; SBN 76).

6.7. KANT'S 'REPLY' TO HUME

Traditionally, Hume's argument to do with the causal inference has been interpreted as thoroughly negative, as showing that inductive inferences are somehow unreasonable or unwarranted or unjustified.[22] The problem with this interpretation is that it is incompatible with many features of Hume's philosophy. If inductive inferences are unwarranted, then so is the whole project of the science of human nature, which is based in the experimental method, an inductive method, indeed, Hume makes inductive inferences constantly, before, during and after the famous argument in both the *Treatise* and *Enquiry*.[23] As Baier succinctly puts it, 'if Hume really *distrusts* the causal inference. . .then he must distrust his own *Treatise*' (1991: 55). Recent trends in Hume scholarship have rejected interpreting Hume's argument as a claim about the justification of these inferences, interpreting the argument instead as an explanation of how the inference is produced. Garrett argues that 'Hume's conclusion. . .concerns the causation of inductive inferences. . .rather than the justification of such inferences (1997: 94). Owen claims that Hume's conclusion is not that probable reasoning is unreasonable but that the 'activity of probable reasoning cannot be explained by traditional theories of reason' (1999: 137–8). This argument is not concerned 'with the question of. . .whether the conclusions of probable reasoning are justified, but with the question of how we come by beliefs in the unobserved *at all*, so the problem is how the beliefs are produced not how they are justified (1999: 137f).

This recent trend in scholarship seems compatible with Kant's own interpretation of Hume's account of the causal inference. In the *Prolegomena to Any Future Metaphysics*, Kant chastises Hume's critics for not recognizing that the argument concerned not the *warrant* but the *origin* of the causal inference. He notes that Hume suffered the 'usual misfortune' of being misunderstood by his critics and goes on to argue that his critics erred because they took for granted what he doubted and demonstrated 'with zeal and often with impudence' what he never thought of doubting (PR 5). The problem Hume faced was not whether the concept of cause was right, useful or indispensable. 'Hume's problem', according to Kant, concerned the origin of the concept of cause, particularly, whether the concept could be 'thought by reason *a priori*', thereby 'implying a wider application then merely to objects of experience' (PR 5). Hume was to know exactly how it is possible that 'when a concept is given [to him], [he] can go beyond it and connect with it another. . .as if the latter necessarily belonged to the former' (PR 28). And, as Kant rightly points out in the *Critique of Pure Reason*, Hume thought that, 'no faculty of understanding can lead us from the concept of a thing to the existence of something else which is thereby universally and necessarily given' (CPR A765/B793).

Now while Kant famously credits Hume with interrupting his 'dogmatic slumber' and giving his 'investigation in the field of speculative philosophy quite a new direction', he was 'far from following him in the conclusions at which he arrived' (PR 7). He allowed that Hume 'demonstrated irrefutably that it was entirely impossible for reason to think *a priori* and by means of concepts [the] combination [of which] involves necessity', but thought that on Hume's own positive account the concept of cause and effect becomes 'nothing but a bastard of imagination, impregnated by experience' (PR 4, 28). Kant thought that if the concept is derived Hume's way, then the requirements of necessity and universality, central to the concept of cause and effect, are utterly lost (CPR A196/B241). He says that he first tried to put Hume's objection in a more general form and discovered that the concept of a strict connection between cause and effect is not the only idea by which the understanding 'thinks the connexion of things *a priori*' but rather that 'metaphysics consisted altogether of such connexions' (PR 7). He goes on to say that he 'succeeded in solving Hume's problem not merely in the particular case, but respect to the whole faculty of pure reason' (PR 8, 73). The proper work of philosophy becomes making explicit the inner connections between these rules that govern our thought and action. Kant's idea was that the mind was the source of rules which it imposes on the raw material of experience. This would establish that principles like 'every event has a cause' as necessary and universal because they are part of an inbuilt framework with which we structure experience. Causation becomes a necessary structural feature or condition of experience.

The Second Analogy in the *Critique of Pure Reason* is intended to show that 'Everything that happens. . .presupposes something upon which it follows according to a rule' (CPR A188) and that 'all alterations occur in accordance with the law of connection of cause and effect' (CPR B232). Now in accordance with such a rule, Kant argues, 'there must. . .lie in that which in general precedes an occurrence the condition for a rule, in accordance with which this occurrence always and necessarily follows' (CPR A193/B238). He claims that his transcendental solution gives us the right cognize the law of connection *a priori*. By way of example, he continues 'if wax that was previously firm melts, I can cognize *a priori* that something must have preceded (e.g., the warmth of the sun) on which this has followed in accordance with a constant law' (CPR A766/B794). Now if causes and effects act in accordance with a constant law of connection, then on this model the same effects will invariably follow from the same causes.

Kant clarifies his position with the difference between a subjective and an objective order with the famous house and ship examples (A190–193/B235–238). Suppose that we have a sequence of impressions of a stationary object, for example, a house. We can look first at the roof, then at the middle, and finally at the ground floor. This sequence of impressions can easily be reversed; I merely have to look at the house in the opposite order, from bottom to top. The point is that in this case we do not count the sequence of impressions as constituting an order that is objective; instead, it is merely subjective, reflecting only the order of perceptions. In contrast, consider the successive impressions we have of a ship as it passes in front of us. We have an impression first higher up in the stream, then a little lower down, then farther down. The sequence of impressions exemplifies an order of perceptions that we are constrained to regard as determined or irreversible, reflecting an objective order among the objects perceived. In the house example, no such objective causal relations tie down the order involved in the perception of the house. Kant's point is that we cannot draw this distinction between the objective order of things and a subjective order unless we antecedently possess the idea of an objective order.

On Henry Allison's influential interpretation of Kant's argument, the irreversibility thesis, illustrated by the ship example, characterizes the way in which we connect perceptions in thought, if we are to experience '*through* them an objective succession'.[24] Irreversibility thus refers to the conceptual ordering of the pure understanding through which the thought of an object is necessarily determined. The condition under which we think the order of perceptions is irreversible is supplied by an *a priori* rule and it is only by subjecting our perceptions to this rule that we can experience the objective succession of events. So, in the case of event-perception, we regard the order in which perceptions are apprehended as irreversible and this irreversibility results from subjecting the succession of perceptions to an *a priori* rule, which specifies how any cognizer confronted with this sequence ought to construe it.[25]

Kant makes this point in the Second Analogy when he attempts to show that 'even in experience we never ascribe sequence. . .to the object and distinguish it from the subjective sequence of our apprehension, except when a rule is the ground that necessitates us to observe this order of the perceptions rather than another' (CPR A196–7/B241–2). He goes to say that it is 'really this necessitation that first makes possible the representation of a succession in the object' (CPR A196–7/B241–2). He elaborates on this through the general question of how 'we come to posit an object for [our mere] representations', that is, how we ascribe 'some sort of objective reality' to the mere 'subjective reality' of our representations (CPR A197/B242). Kant's answer is that the 'characteristic. . .given to our representations by [their] relation to an object' is that of 'making the combination of representations necessary in a certain way, and subjecting them to a rule' (CPR A197/B242). In other words, the feature distinguishing objective representations from subjective representations is that the former are subject to an *a priori* rule and the latter are not. Consequently, Kant claims that,

> as soon as I perceive or anticipate that there is in this sequence a relation to the preceding state, from which the representation

follows in accordance with a rule, I represent something as an occurrence, or as something that happens, i.e., I cognize an object that I must place in time in a determinate position, which, after the preceding state, cannot be otherwise assigned to it (CPR A198/B243).

One possible response from Hume might consist of a reminder that we easily can and do conceive alternatives to the laws of cause and effect which Kant held to be the necessary conditions of cognizing.[26] As we saw in Chapter 6.2–3, Hume argues it is entirely possible to conceive of something existing without a cause and it is entirely possible to conceive that the course of nature may change and that causes like those we have previously experienced, may be attended with different effects. Now if Kant's theory were correct, surely we would not be able to conceive otherwise. We could not conceive of such things like alternatives to the law of cause and effect because of the *a priori* rule that 'necessitates us to observe this order of the perceptions rather than another' (CPR A196–7/B241–2), or constrains us to regard the order of our perceptions as 'determined'.[27] Further since causality is an *a priori* rule which makes possible connections between perceptions, it would seem not only that we would be unable to conceive of alternatives to the law of cause and effect, but also that we would never be able to make a mistake in our judgments about these sorts of causal relationships.[28] This is because of Kant's suggestion that the slightest hint of its relevance, the mere thought or anticipation of a causal sequence, implies that the *a priori* rule is already present in full force. The mere thought of some causal sequence might be in the object means that it is so in the object, since that thought would not be possible if the sequence in question were merely subjective.

Now the difficulty is that people frequently err in their claims of causal connections. Generally, mistaken claims of causal connection are based on experiences of coincidences: two events closely connected in time which seem causally related but are in fact not. This is easy to do, for as Hume pointed out, in the production of almost any effect, there is a complication of circumstances, some of which are essential to the effect, and some of which, although frequently conjoined with the essential circumstances, are superfluous or coincidental. The superfluous factors, however, may still have an effect on our judgment. Any decent theory of causation must be capable of distinguishing coincidences from genuine causes and currently it is difficult to see how Kant's theory can give an account of this. On Kant's view, all coincidences would end up being treated as genuine causes because we could not even think, 'well, maybe A caused B' unless A had actually caused B.

Hume may well have an advantage here. Aware that we often make mistakes in our causal judgments, he carefully distinguished between accidental and genuine causal instances, that's why in the *Treatise* he supplements his account of causation by offering eight rules to help us determine when objects really do lie in the relation of cause and effect (see Chapter 6.6). The rules help to exclude accidental circumstances in the description of causal relations,[29] and by reflecting on them, 'we learn to distinguish the accidental circumstances from the efficacious causes' (THN 1.3.13.11; SBN 149). When it comes to the issue of accounting for human error and distinguishing between accidental from genuinely causal instances, Hume's theory of causation certainly appears more useful, recognizing the need for fallible beings to actively revise and improve their causal reasonings by offering reasonable guidelines by which to assess and regulate them.

NOTES

1 THN 1.3.2.3; SBN 74; AB 4; SBN 647.
2 For a recent catalogue of responses, see Howson (2000: chapter 1).
3 There is an enormous body of literature on this issue. For a comprehensive bibliography, see Guyer (1992) and Beck (1978).
4 It has recently been suggested that it does not make sense to ask the question of whether Kant successfully replied to Hume because the two have such different models of causality, See Watkins (2004: 449–88).
5 For a thorough discussion of the seven relations, see Owen (1999: 83f).
6 I owe thanks here to Eric Steinberg for helpful comments on presenting Hume's account of relations.
7 EHU 4.4; SBN 26; THN 1.3.2.2–3; SBN 74.
8 This presentation of Hume's fork owes much to notes taken from a lecture by Don Garrett in a modern philosophy seminar at the University of North Carolina at Chapel Hill, fall 2001.
9 THN 1.3.2.6–7; SBN 75–6. Hume acknowledges that it is possible that an effect could be co-temporary with its cause. However, he argues that experience mostly contradicts this and establishes the relation of priority by 'a kind of inference or reasoning'. His argument is based on an 'establish'd maxim both in natural and moral philosophy', a maxim which turns up at 1.3.15 as the eighth rule in the 'Rules by which to judge causes and effects', THN 1.3.2.7; SBN 76.

10 See Hobbes' *Leviathan* (1994: 63).
11 For a classic critique of Hume's argument, see Anscombe (1981: 160). See also Stroud (1977: 46f.).
12 This point is well made by Kemp Smith (1941: 407).
13 Grieg (1932: 187). For more on the reception of Hume's critique of the causal maxim, see Waxman (1994: 141–50).
14 THN; SBN 95; AB 18; SBN 653.
15 The ensuing discussion in this paragraph is indebted to Owen (1999: 155f.).
16 See also THN 1.3.8.15; SBN 105, and 1.3.10.3; SBN 119–20.
17 THN 1.3.7.8; SBN 97–8; EHU 5.2.12; SBN 50.
18 THN 1.3.11.2; SBN 124; EHU 6.n10; SBN 56n.
19 THN 1.3.11.2; SBN 124; EHU 6.n10; SBN 56n.
20 I owe this interpretation of Hume's rules to Garrett (1997: 145).
21 Here I am indebted to Thomas Hearn (1970: 405–422, section I).
22 This interpretation comes in many varieties; probably the classic rendering of this interpretation comes from Stove (1973).
23 Garrett (1997: 78f.). See also Baier (1991: chapter 3), Owen (1999, chapter 6) and Stanistreet (2002: chapter 3).
24 See Allison (2004: 251).
25 See Allison (2004: 252).
26 Howson (2000: 18) suggested this response also.
27 Allison (2004: 250).
28 I am indebted here from discussions with J. Colmon, who first helped me to articulate this objection to Kant's theory.
29 For more on Hume's distinction between accidental versus genuine causes, see Coventry (2006: chapter 5).

CHAPTER 7

NECESSARY CONNECTION

Hume's analysis of a necessary connection between cause and effect is generally thought to be the most significant and influential single contribution to the topic.[1] However, despite the widely recognized importance of his analysis, there is still virtually no agreement amongst commentators about the upshot of his theory. This chapter follows Hume's famous search for the impression of necessary connection, and then explains the application of the resulting doctrine of necessity to the case of human motive and action and its importance for morality and religion. Finally, I evaluate current 'realist' and 'anti-realist' interpretative trends to do with Hume's account of causation and contribute a third interpretation into the debate.[2]

7.1. THE IDEA OF NECESSARY CONNECTION

So far, we learnt that cause and effect inferences have three stages. First, there is a present impression or vivid ideas of memory. Second, there is an inference based on contiguity, succession and constant conjunction. Third, there is a communication of vivacity from the first impression or vivid idea of memory to the inferred idea. The communication of vivacity explains why we believe the inferred idea and why the inferred idea has an influence on behavior. Hume goes on to expand on the different types of causal reasoning, and even presents rules to regulate these reasonings. The next step is to tackle the most important element in the causal relation, that of a necessary connection. According to Hume, there are no ideas in metaphysics more obscure and uncertain than those of power, force, energy, and necessary connection. In the *Treatise*, he treats necessary connexion as synonymous with efficacy, agency and productive quality (THN

1.3.14; SBN 157) and it is his endeavor to fix the 'precise' meanings of these words (EHU 7.1.3; SBN 62). His understanding of a necessary connection between cause and effect is indebted to Malebranche (see Chapter 2.3.2). Both believe that the crucial component of our idea of cause involves the perception of a necessary connection and that the necessary connection is a connection by which the effect must follow necessarily from the cause: the cause necessitates the effect and it is impossible that the effect does not follow.

The discussion of necessary connections proceeds with a familiar question: from what impression is our idea of necessary connection derived? (THN 1.3.14.1; SBN 155) The starting point is, therefore, the Copy Principle – this will be the guide to uncovering the idea of necessary connection. One place to look for the impression would be the operations of causes and effects in the external world. However, there is nothing in any particular instance of cause and effect involving external objects which suggests the idea of power or necessary connection. It is impossible therefore that we can derive the idea of power from external objects (EHU 7.1.6–9; SBN 63–4; THN 1.3.14.10; SBN 164). When we examine a single case of two events we regard as causally related, our impressions are only of their conjunction, contiguity and priority; there is no experience of their necessary connection. When we go beyond the single case to examine the background of experienced constant conjunctions of similar pairs of events, there is little to add, for 'there is nothing in a number of instances, different from every single instance, which is supposed to be exactly similar' (EHU 7.2.28; SBN 75).

The most 'general and popular' theory of power derived from experience at the time came from Locke (THN 1.3.14.5; SBN 157). Locke thought that the idea of causal power between objects was developed after the experience of repeated instances of change in external objects, and the subsequent alteration in our simple ideas. This means that whenever we observe a change, the mind 'collects a Power' able to make 'that Change, as well as a possibility in the thing it self to receive it' (ECHU 2.22.4). The idea of power thus is a *postulation* underlying the observed relationship between causes and effects in the natural world. Hume renounces the role assigned to reason insisting that reason can never be the origin of the idea of power.[3] He goes on to say that if we are to have a just idea of power we must discover it through the legitimate source: experience (THN 1.3.14.6; SBN 157–8).

The prospects for an intelligible account of power derived from experience are not good when one considers the many competing accounts (THN 1.3.14.7; SBN 158). Philosophers sensible of this difficulty conclude that they do not know what the power or efficacy in nature is, and some of these philosophers, such as the Cartesians, followers of Descartes, think that matter is wholly inactive and thus contains none of the power or efficacy associated with causes and their effects. According to these philosophers, the essence of matter consists in extension, which implies only mobility and not the production, continuation or communication of motion (THN 1.3.14.8–9; SBN 159). Since they can never discover the ultimate force in nature, they conclude that God must be responsible for the changes which occur in matter. This had been put forward not only by Descartes but also by Malebranche, who argued that power does not reside in nature but in the volition of the Supreme Being. God is the true and direct cause of every effect is not power or force in nature but the volition of God who wills that these objects be connected forever with each other and the immediate cause of the union between soul and body. Hume challenges this alternative on the ground that every idea is derived from some impression. We have no impression of God, so we can have no clear idea of God as the source of the power in the universe, so appealing to God's causality cannot increase our understanding of necessary connection either. Just as we are ignorant of the powers that operate between objects, we are equally ignorant of the force by which God operates on the causes and effects in nature and the union between the soul and the body.[4] Hume also argues that such conclusions lead us beyond the operations of human reason and represents irresponsible speculation (EHU 7.1.24; SBN 72).

Hume turns to the operation of our own minds to see if the idea is copied from an internal impression, by reflecting on the operations of our own minds. In particular, he has two cases in mind: the command exercised by the will to:

(i) Move the organs of the body, and
(ii) Direct the faculties of the mind (EHU 7.1.9; SBN 64).

Locke thought that reflecting on the powers of the mind involved in voluntary action provided us with the clearest idea of power (ECHU 2.21.4). When we reflect on the operations of our minds, he argues, we do perceive the causal power itself; in particular, we observe in ourselves 'a *Power* to begin or forbear, continue or end several actions of our minds and motions of our Bodies' (ECHU 2.21.5; 2.23.20). He calls this power of the mind the 'Will', while any exercise of that power is called 'Willing' or 'Volition' and any action which is performed consequent to the command of the mind is voluntary while any action performed without a command from the mind is deemed involuntary.

Hume counters that we are ignorant of the power of the will to move the body or the mind and concludes that our idea of power is not copied from any impression of power copied from within ourselves.[5] He offers three arguments against each possibility. Of the former, he argues that there is nothing more mysterious than the union of the soul and body. But if we perceived the power of the will, then we would know the connexion between the mind and the body but we don't. Second, we do not have an influence over all parts of our body, we can move our tongues and fingers, but not our heart or liver. If we were conscious of a power, then we would know why the will can influence some parts but not others, but we don't so we are not conscious of power. Third, anatomy teaches that the immediate object of power in voluntary action is not the member moved but certain muscles, nerves and animal spirits, and perhaps something even more unknown. Because we do not know precisely what the presumed power of the mind to move the body is actually doing, we have proof that the power on which this operation is performed is completely unintelligible (EHU 7.1.10–15; SBN 66).

He dismisses next the view that we are conscious of a power, when by the act of our own will we raise up an idea. This will not do because when we know a power, we know the circumstance in the cause, by which it is enabled to produce the effect. But, we don't know the nature of the human soul or the nature of an idea nor how the one produces the others. Second, the command of the mind over itself is limited, like the case of the body; our authority over our passions and sentiments is much weaker than over our ideas. But, we don't know why the power is limited in one case and not the other. If we saw the power, however, we would know. Third, self-command is different at different times. For example, some people have better control of their thoughts in the morning than in the evening. We cannot give any reason for these variations except by experience, there is certainly no power of which we are conscious so we must conclude that the power is beyond our comprehension (EHU 7.1.16–19; SBN 68).

Overall, a careful examination of the operations between causes and effects as they appear to the senses supplies no impression, either external or internal, that suggests an idea of power. Since the idea of necessary connection is a general term, it follows that, for Hume, it is an abstract idea, so since we have an idea of it, there must be some particular instance of it observable to us:

> It has been establish'd as a certain principle, that general or abstract ideas are nothing but individual ones taken in a certain light. . .If we be possest, therefore, of any idea of power in general, we must also be able to conceive some particular species of it (THN 1.3.14.13; SBN 161).

He goes on to argue that there can be no idea of power as it resides in external objects because we can never 'conceive how any particular power can possibly reside in any particular object' (THN 1.3.14.13; SBN 162). Since general or abstract are only 'individual ones taken in a certain light', it follows that 'we deceive ourselves in imagining we can form any such general idea' of power or necessary connection (THN 1.3.14.13; SBN 161–2). The point is that the idea of power would have to come from that of a specific case of it, but we cannot find an instance of power in the objects of the world or in the internal operations of the mind.

Every idea is derived from an impression. There is no simple impression of necessity which can be discovered. The idea of necessity is produced, not discovered from the repeated observation of the constant conjunction of certain impressions across many resembling instances. The repetition produces nothing new in the objects but something new in the mind of the observer. The necessary connexion between cause and effect, by which we believe that one event infallibly causes another, derives from something we *feel* in the mind. After several observations of constant conjunction, the mind is carried by habit upon the appearance of one event to expect its usual attendant, and we pronounce events to be connected (EHU 7.2.27–8; SBN 75). So we observe event *A* followed by *B* and after repeated instances of such an observation, we start to infer *B* on the appearance of *A*. For Hume, the necessary connection between cause and effect is a habit of the mind, built from the faculty of imagination. This feeling of determination in the mind then is the 'essence of necessity' (THN 1.3.14.22; SBN 165). When we say that two objects are necessarily connected, we mean nothing more that that 'they have acquired a connexion in our thought' (EHU 7.2.28; SBN 76).

Hume is aware that the view advanced may be received unfavorably because it reverses the order of nature by placing necessity in the mind and not in the objects. He accounts for the bias by noting that we *project* our feeling of anticipation onto the observed events, under the mistaken impression that we are experiencing a necessary connection that inheres in the events themselves. We feel a customary connection between the ideas in the imagination, and we transfer that feeling to objects. The mind thus has a 'great propensity to spread itself on external objects', and 'this same propensity is the reason why we suppose necessity and power to lie in the objects' (THN 1.3.14.25; SBN 167).[6] In the *Enquiry*, he puts the point this way: 'we *feel* a customary connexion between the ideas, we transfer that feeling to the objects' (EHU 7.2.n17; SBN 78n).[7]

Hume ends the discussion by forming two definitions of cause and effect, one as a philosophical and the other as a natural relation.[8] First, a cause is defined as: 'An object precedent and contiguous to another, and where all the objects resembling the former are plac'd in like relations of precedency and contiguity to those objects, that resemble the latter' (THN 1.3.14.31; SBN 170; EHU 7.2.29; SBN 76). In the *Enquiry*, he recasts the first definition an 'object, followed by another, where all the objects similar to the first are followed by objects similar to the second', adding a counterfactual twist, 'If the first object had not been the second never had existed' (EHU 7.2.29; SBN 76). Second, a cause is: 'an object precedent and contiguous to another, and so united with it, that the idea of the one determines the mind to form the idea of the other, and the impression of the one to form a more lively idea of the other' (THN 1.3.14.31; SBN 170; EHU 7.2.29; SBN 77). The first definition points to features of events contributed by the natural world, and the second definition records a spectator's reaction or response to those events.[9]

7.2. LIBERTY AND NECESSITY

In both the *Treatise* and the *Enquiry*, Hume applies his account of necessity to the case of human motive and action and outlines its implications for morality and religion. There are important differences between the two accounts however. In the *Treatise*, Hume was concerned to attack defenders of liberty, however in the *Enquiry*, he adopts a more conciliatory approach by attempting to reconcile the doctrines of liberty and necessity, characterizing the dispute as merely verbal that will dissolve once we have grasped the proper meanings of the words.

He rehearses his doctrine of necessity. It is universally acknowledged that the operations of external bodies are necessary; they are governed by necessary connections. In no instance can the ultimate connection be discovered, either by senses or reason, we observe only the constant conjunction of objects. Our idea of necessity is the determination of the mind to pass from one object to its usual attendant. These two parts are essential to necessity, the constant union and the inference of the mind, represented by the two definitions of a cause.

Following the doctrine of necessity, he argues. The doctrine of necessity takes place in the voluntary actions of human beings. Therefore, there is a necessity in human behavior. That certain motives produce actions that have the same causal necessity that we observe in external objects. As to the first part of necessity, Hume argues that it also universally acknowledged that there is a great uniformity among the actions of humans, the same motives produce the same actions, just as the same events follow from the same causes. History informs us of the constant and uniform principles of human nature, we get a variety of circumstances, furnishing us with the materials, from which we form our observations and learn about human behavior. Some examples include the records of wars, factions, revolutions, and so on, are collections of principles by which the politician and philosopher fixes the principles of their science just as the natural philosophers study plants and minerals and other external objects and forms experiments concerning them. We also become acquainted with the regularities of human behavior by long life experience engaging in a variety of businesses and company, instructing us of the principles of human nature. We gain knowledge of people's motives and inclinations from actions, expressions, gestures, and then interpret them with what we know about their motives. These general observations teach us about human nature.

Were there no uniformity in actions, it would be impossible to collect any general observations of human action, so politics and morals as sciences would be impossible because they depend on the regularities of human behavior. Hume warns that he does not expect that people in the same circumstances will always act precisely in the same manner, there are, after all, diversity of characters, opinions, prejudices, not to mention the issue of the manners of humans in different countries and ages. But, after observing a variety of conduct in different people and differing circumstances, we are able to form a variety of maxims which suppose a degree of uniformity. We draw inferences concerning human actions and those inferences are founded on the experienced union of like actions with like motives, characters and circumstances. Thus, the union between motive and action possesses the same constancy which we observe between cause and effect in the physical operations. This constancy influences the understanding in the same way that constant conjunction in physical operations influences the understanding, by determining us to infer the existence of one from that of another. He grants it is possible that we can find some actions that do not have a regular connection with motives and are exceptions to regular conduct. The most irregular actions are frequently accounted for when you know more about character and situation. A person with a nice reputation snaps at you, but it turns that they have not eaten or they have a headache. An action which seems irregular thus can be subsumed under another regularity about behavior.

The connection between motive and action is therefore necessary in the same way that the operations of nature are relevant. It is from experience that we draw inferences concerning the future and it is the same experience of human actions which is the source from which we draw inferences. Understood this way, human action is no different from any other kind of action in nature. In both cases, we find constant conjunctions which induce us to believe that future patterns of activity will resemble those past. Our liberty consists in the power of acting or not acting, according to the determinations of the will, which in turn produces actions – if we choose to move, we may, if we choose to rest, we may. This belongs to everyone who is not forcibly constrained. Hume thinks the will is the impression we feel as we consciously move a body part or a new perception in the mind (THN 2.3.1.2; SBN 399). All mental or physical actions produced by the will arise from antecedent motives, tempers, and circumstances and there is an observed constant conjunction between the existence of certain desires or motives and the carrying out of certain actions (THN 2.3.1.5; SBN 401). This doctrine of liberty is

similar to Locke's, i.e., that liberty is lack of external co
(ECHU 2.21.6). This sort of liberty is sometimes referred t
liberty of spontaneity, a freedom from physical constr
opposed to a *liberty of indifference*, which is a negation of causes
where the will is undetermined by anything but its own choice. Locke
and Hume differ however in their explanations of what exactly the
'power' of the will is. Locke thought that the experience of the will
was a direct experience of power (see Chapter 7.1) whereas Hume
denies we experience a power within us, opting instead for observed
constant conjunctions between motive and action.

People have disagreed about the doctrines of necessity and
liberty because people are generally ambivalent in their views on
necessity (EHU 8.1.22; SBN 93). Some people think that we can
penetrate further into nature and see a necessary connection
between cause and effect. When we turn to reflecting on the operations of our own mind, we don't think that the same connection
between motive and action exists. So it is mistakenly supposed that
there is a difference between the operations of matter and those
which arise from thought. But when we admit that we know
nothing more about causation apart from the two definitions, we
can ascribe the same necessity to all causes and it can take place in
voluntary actions.

7.3. MORAL AND RELIGIOUS IMPLICATIONS OF NECESSITY

Hume defends his account further by arguing that it is consistent
with morality, but also essential for supporting morality (EHU 8.2).
The doctrine of necessity is consistent with morality because morality is founded on rewards and punishments. That is, the threat of
punishments and the hope of rewards are supposed to influence
human behavior. How can we expect rewards and punishments to
influence people if there is no necessary connection among humans'
motives and actions? The denial of necessity would undercut moral
assessment, for such assessments presuppose that actions are
causally linked to motives, that your motives can influence your
actions. On this view, we can never blame any person for their
actions, for if you didn't cause it, then how can you be responsible
for it?[10]

Liberty in his sense of the word is necessary for morality because
no human action where it is lacking can be praised or blamed.

Actions caused by external forces excuse the agent from moral responsibility. This is because in circumstances when external forces cause the action, we cannot make an inference to the person's motive. It is only when an action is believed to be determined by the will of the agent that the agent is deemed an object of praise and blame. In fact, as Russell points out, in cases of external forces, it is psychologically impossible to hold the agent responsible.[11] This has to do with Hume's view that approval and disapproval are essential to morality and that only character traits or mental qualities arouse our moral sentiments of approval or disapproval.[12] Hume thinks that the mind is formed by nature to feel the sentiment of praise or blame upon the appearance of certain characters, dispositions and actions. To hold someone responsible is to feel this sentiment psychologically. So, if someone does something wrong to me, then I hold that person responsible and feel the sentiment of blame directed at that person. Knowledge of a person's character traits or mental qualities requires inference. A person is held responsible if we regard them as an object of moral sentiment. Regarding an agent responsible is a matter of feeling not judgment. Without inference to character, without supposing that the action is caused by a person's motives, passions or states of character, no such feeling could, as a matter of psychological fact, be aroused in us and therefore no one could be regarded as responsible. The upshot is that without liberty and necessity, morality would be impossible.

In the last part of the discussion of liberty and necessity in the *Enquiry*, Hume points out two implications of necessity for religion. If everything proceeds according to necessary causes and if God is the ultimate cause of the universe, then everything in the universe, including our volitions and actions, is caused by God. This appears to present a dilemma for those who believe in God. For if God ultimately causes our motives, then one of two consequences follow:

(1) No human action can be bad and blamable because God cannot possibly be bad
(2) God is the ultimate cause of all guilt and moral turpitude in human action.

Some philosophers affirm the first horn of the dilemma and suppose that there is no real evil when the world is considered as one whole system ordered with perfect benevolence. This means that every physical ill makes an essential part of this benevolent system and cannot be removed by the deity without giving rise to greater ill or sacrificing the greater good; in other words, this world is the best possible world and has the best balance of evil over good. This is the system of Leibniz.[13] Hume is not satisfied with this. No matter how much our imagination may be pleased by speculative theories about the absence of evil in the world, we still feel the moral sentiments of blame and approbation. A person who is robbed of loads of money will not feel the loss diminished by such reflections and there is no reason why his moral resentment against the crime should be viewed as incompatible; this is simply the natural sentiments of the human mind and these sentiments cannot be affected by philosophical theory or speculation. Such abstract thoughts cannot overcome our feeling that there is not something terribly wrong when one is suffering.

The second horn of the dilemma is much more difficult and Hume in the end pronounces the whole issue a mystery, writing that it exceeds 'the power of philosophy' (EHU 8.36; SBN 103). Essentially, he argues that it is impossible to reconcile the freedom of human actions, thus allowing punishment of bad actions and free God from being the author of sin and thus not perfect. Hume invokes the fourth part of the experimental method, recommending that we leave such uncertainties alone and return to the proper province of human reason: the examination of common life.

7.4. THE IMAGINARY STANDARD OF A NECESSARY CONNECTION

Hume's doctrine of necessary connections has invoked much disagreement amongst scholars.[14] Recently, it has become popular to characterize Hume's theory of causation as a brand of causal realism. Wright and Galen Strawson are prominent amongst those commentators who defend causal realist interpretations of Hume's theory.[15] Their readings are not exactly similar, but both share the view that (i) while he denies we can have any knowledge of causal powers or forces or necessary connections in external objects, (ii) he certainly believes that such things really do exist in external objects; indeed, it never even occurred to him to deny the existence of such things.

Wright claims that Hume's theory of causation assumes a fundamental belief in the existence of objective necessary causal powers in the objects, although he maintains firmly at the same time that we can know nothing about them, and can never hope to understand anything of their nature. Indeed, he argues that one misses the central aim of Hume's philosophy unless one recognizes that 'he consistently maintained the point of view that there are real powers and forces in nature which are not directly accessible to our senses'.[16] He thinks that there is no doubt that causation is more than just regular succession in objects for Hume, even though we can never have a genuine understanding of exactly what that necessary connection between cause and effect might be.[17] According to Wright, our natural instincts lead us to posit the existence of necessary connections, forces, or powers between external objects and between the mind and the body. He writes that: 'By yielding to the authority of natural instinct Hume was led to affirm a real power and necessary connection in the relations of the mind and body, and also in purely physical events'.[18] In fact, our natural instincts confirm both the independent and unperceived existence of external objects, and the existence of objective necessary connections between objects; he claims that 'Custom leads us to suppose the existence of a causal power inherent in the objects of the senses, whether they may be the immediate objects, or the independent unperceived external objects'.[19] The belief in causal power, according to Wright's Hume, is a belief in an intelligible or conceptual connection between the cause and effect. This type of connection is such that if the idea of it were available to the mind, the effect could be inferred *a priori* from the cause.[20] Unfortunately, the mind has no idea of such connections because we never observe them, so the idea of cause and effect that the mind actually possesses is inadequate to its object.

Strawson distinguishes between ontological and epistemological levels in Hume's philosophy. On the ontological level, Hume proceeds on the assumption that real causal powers or ultimate forces which bind events together exist in nature; indeed, it never even occurred to him to doubt their existence.[21] The only thing that Hume was concerned to deny is that we can have any *knowledge* of such ultimate forces.[22] On the epistemological level, all we can know about causation in the objects is just regular succession because the circumstance in the cause, which gives its connection with the effect, is entirely concealed from us. Nonetheless, he believes that the regular succession observed is a manifestation of a definite and true causal power that exists in nature, although 'we know nothing of its nature and have no sort of positive conception of it'.[23] To believe in causal power, according to Strawson's Hume, is to believe 'that there must be and is something about reality given which is ordered and regular on the way that it is' or to believe 'in there being something about reality in virtue of which it is regular in the way that it is'.[24] According to Strawson then, Hume believes in the existence of causal powers because he just thinks that there must be some reason why things in the world are regular in the way that they are.

Both Wright and Strawson have many arguments in favor of their realist interpretation. Each have argued that Hume allows a 'relative' idea of necessary connections between objects: it is whatever it is that underpins the regular succession we observe in nature or whatever it is that forces those regularities we observe to occur. Strawson argues that the 'relative' idea of necessary connection suffices for Hume, 'in such a way that we can go on to refer to it while having descriptively contentful conception of its nature on the terms of his theory of ideas'.[25] This argument makes use of a 'supposing versus conceiving' distinction that occurs marginally in another part of his work (in the discussion of our idea of an external world). The idea is that we can legitimately suppose that certain things exist, such as necessary connections in objects, even when we strictly have no clear idea of what it is that we are supposing.[26] This is possible, according to Wright, because Hume did not adhere to the 'theory of ideas, strictly and literally interpreted'.[27] Attention is also drawn to Hume's use of realist-sounding forms of expression that abound particularly in Section 4 of the *Enquiry*, as evidence that Hume takes for granted the existence of necessary connections in the world.[28] For example, there is his frequent use of such terms as 'secret powers', 'secret causes', 'ultimate causes', 'those powers, forces, or principles upon which the regular succession of objects totally depends', and 'the ultimate force and efficacy of nature'.

These arguments have been met with numerous objections in the literature: it has been emphasized that the supposing versus conceiving distinction is never used in the analysis of causation, and that the distinction never appears in the later *Enquiry* at all. It has also been suggested that his use of apparently realist expressions such as 'secret powers' are ironic or are not intended to be genuinely referential.[29] I am not going to settle all these issues here, but I do think that there are at least two serious problems in making a belief in causal powers or necessary connections in nature fundamental to his philosophy of causation. First, Hume's positive explanation of necessary connections between causes and effects pointedly includes no mention of powers or forces in objects. Hume's discussion of liberty and necessity is helpful on this point. When recapitulating his view of necessity, Hume writes that the constant union of events and the consequent inference of the mind represented by the two definitions of a cause are 'essential to necessity' (THN 2.3.1.4; SBN 400). These two particulars 'form the whole of that necessity, which we ascribe to matter' and that beyond them 'we have no notion of any necessity or connexion' (EHU 8.1.5; SBN 82 and AB 34; SBN 660f.).[30] If realist interpretations were correct, we would expect him to add something like, 'apart from, of course, the wonderful and infallible power which we never experience, but nonetheless posit to explain the regularities we experience'. Instead, Hume tells us that the actions of matter have no necessity but that of a constant union of objects and the determination of the mind to pass from the cause to the effect (THN 2.3.1.4; SBN 400). Moreover, he states that this customary transition in the imagination is 'the same with the power and necessity; which are consequently qualities of perceptions, not of objects' (THN 1.3.14.24; SBN 166).

Not only does Hume emphasize carefully and often that the idea of a necessary connection between cause and effect exists in the mind only, and not in the objects, but he also argues that we engage in error if we continue to believe that the necessary connection actually exists in the objects. For example, in the *Treatise* after claiming that the 'real power of causes' 'belongs entirely to the soul' (THN 1.3.14.23; SBN 166), he writes that we are led astray by a 'false philosophy' when 'we transfer the determination of the thought to external objects, and suppose any real intelligible connexion betwixt them' (THN 1.3.14.27; SBN 168). When we speak of a necessary connection between objects while supposing that such a thing depends on the objects themselves and not our own minds, 'in all these expressions, *so apply'd*, we really have no distinct meaning, and make use of common words, without any clear and determinate ideas' (THN 1.3.14.14; SBN 162). Using terms like power, force, or necessary connection while at the same time assuming these terms depend on something objectively inheres in objects is illegitimate. The necessary connection is a quality which is drawn from what we feel internally and thus, 'can *only* belong to the mind that considers them' (THN 1.3.14.27; SBN 168; my emphasis). To attribute to

Hume a belief in powers or necessary connections of the type described by realist interpretations would be to go against exactly what he advises in his philosophy of causation, which makes causal realism an unappealing interpretive option. Rather, causal anti-realist interpretations, which deny powers or forces in objects a place in his system of causation, begin to look like a more promising alternative.

Causal anti-realist interpretations come in two types: regularity theories and projectivist theories. According to the former, he holds that statements of causal connection are reducible to statements of constant conjunction. The reduction of causation to regular succession or constant conjunction means that he denies either (i) that causes are necessarily connected, or (ii) that causation even exists, or (iii) that the very notion of causal power has any meaning.

John Leland, Richard Taylor, and A. H. Basson all hold the first view. In 1757, Leland writes that, according to Hume, experience reveals only a 'mere conjunction of events', consequently, 'there is no such thing as necessary connection, or indeed any connection at all, betwixt cause and effect'.[31] Taylor argues that Hume proposed to eliminate necessity from the concept of causation altogether, 'maintaining essentially that causes and effects are merely changes that we find constantly conjoined', that is, 'to say that A was the cause of B provided A was immediately followed by B and that things similar to A are always followed by things similar to B'.[32] In a similar fashion, Basson takes Hume to be attempting to explain how people are mistaken in supposing that causation involves necessary connections in addition to a uniform sequence of events.[33] As an instance of the second, Ernest Mach argues that Hume reduced causality to the 'mere constant conjunction of successive sensations' and that in doing so he 'reject[ed] causality and recognize[d] only a wonted succession in time'.[34] Third, Thomas Reid argues that Hume thought that we had no idea of power at all and that words like 'powers', or 'necessary connexions' were completely without meaning, allowing only 'a constant conjunction of that which we call the cause with the effect'.[35]

In defense of their interpretation, regularity theory supporters need only point to Hume's first definition of a cause. Regularity theory defenders may also point to many statements made in both the *Treatise* and the *Enquiry*, which appear to outright deny any possibility of an idea of power or necessary connection. For example, he writes that, 'since we can never distinctly conceive how any particular power can possibly reside in any particular object, we deceive ourselves in imagining we can form any such general idea' (THN 1.3.14.14; SBN 162). And,

> All events seem entirely loose and separate. One event follows another; but we never can observe any tie between them. They seem *conjoined*, but never *connected*. And as we can have no idea of any thing which never appeared to our outward sense or inward sentiment, the necessary conclusion *seems* to be that we have no idea of connexion or power at all, and that these words are absolutely without any meaning (EHU 7.2.26; SBN 74).

And finally:

> Every idea is copied from some. . .impression. . .and where we cannot find any impression, we may be certain that there is no idea. In all single instances of the operations of bodies there is nothing that produces any impression, nor consequently can suggest any idea of power or necessary connexion (EHU 7.2.30; SBN 78).[36]

The difficulties associated with regularity theory interpretations have been well documented. Essentially, Hume does not deprive causation of necessary connections, nor does he hold it to be a word without meaning. First, he holds that a fundamental component of the idea of cause and effect is that of necessary connection,[37] in fact, in the *Enquiry*, Hume challenges one to 'define a cause, without comprehending, as a part of the definition, a *necessary connexion* with its effect' (EHU 8.25; SBN 95). He certainly does say that if by 'necessary connexion' or 'power' one means something that exists in the operations of external objects or minds, then these words have no meaning (THN 1.3.14.14; SBN 162). However, this does not mean that the words 'power' or 'necessary connexion' have no meaning at all. It just turns out that these words mean something different that what we might have first thought: powers, forces, energies, and so on, lie not in the external objects but in a feeling of determination in the mind raised by the repeated experience of regular conjunctions between cause and effect. Using words like power or force are then legitimate, just as long as their content is taken to be a claim about regularities between objects, and the effect of the repeated observation of regularities on the human mind. He puts it this way in the Abstract to the *Treatise*: words such as power, force, and energy 'mean. . .that determination of the thought, acquir'd by habit, to pass from the cause to its usual effect' (AB 26; SBN 657). When we say that causes and effects are necessarily connected, we 'mean only that they have acquir'd a connexion in our thought' (EHU 76). Moreover, Hume goes on to utilize his definition of necessity as the constant union of objects and the determination of the mind in his defense of the doctrines of liberty and necessity in both the *Treatise* and the *Enquiry*. Indeed, he tells us firmly that 'we *must* acknowledge a necessity' whenever these two particulars are present (THN 2.3.1.4; SBN 400; my emphasis). On Hume's account then, we do have an idea of a necessary connection, and it is something more than constant conjunction between objects, even if it arises out of the experience of such conjunction.

This leaves the other anti-realist interpretation associated with his position: projectivism. According to this interpretation, Hume holds that necessary causal connections lie solely in a feeling or sentiment in the mind. This feeling of anticipation is *projected* or *transferred* onto the regularly conjoined objects that we observe and this explains why we (mistakenly) think that we experience a power or necessary connection that lies in the events themselves. Since statements about causes involve ascribing to objects qualities that exist not in the object but in our own minds, it is thought once again that he denies that we have an idea of necessary connection and that there is such a connection between cause and effect. According to Lord Kames, for instance, Hume denied that we have an idea of necessary connection. He explains that on his view the 'essence of necessary connection or power upon that propensity which custom produces to pass from an object to the idea of its usual attendant'.[38]

More recently, Stroud has defended this view. He argues that Hume thinks that when we make judgments about causes, morals and aesthetics, we ascribe to objects qualities that exist not in the object but in our own minds. When it comes to necessity between the objects, 'nothing in the world is actually connected with anything else, anywhere'.[39] Hume thus rejects objective necessary connections in the external objects then: such a position is incoherent. The operation of 'gilding or staining' the world with an internal sentiment can 'never really succeed in producing an intelligible thought which attributes certain "added" features to external objects or to the relations between them'.[40]

Stroud goes on to say that Hume implies that we are at best confused in our attempts to think of things as causally connected. According to some defenders of projectivist interpretations, Hume thinks that because our causal statements express feelings or sentiments and do not describe causal powers or necessary connections, they cannot be genuine propositions capable of truth or falsity.[41]

As we have already seen when evaluating causal realist and reductionist interpretations, many, many passages support the view that our causal statements are products of feeling or sentiment. There are his frequent assertions that the necessary connection between cause and effect exists in the mind only and not in the objects.[42] There is also Hume's second definition of a cause, which refers to the determination of the mind: 'an object followed by another, and whose appearance always conveys the thought to that other' (EHU 7.2.29; SBN 77; THN 1.3.14.31; SBN 170). Projectivist interpretations are right to emphasize that causal statements are based on feeling and not on the presence of causal powers; however, I do not think that Hume shows any temptation to the view that there cannot be causal judgments which are genuinely true or false because of their psychological source. Indeed, Hume thought that we are instinctively determined to judge the connections between causes and effects as either true or false in just the same way that I cannot help but squint when I turn my unprotected eyes directly towards the bright light of the sun (THN 1.4.1.7; SBN 183).

There appears to be considerable textual evidence for, but also considerable textual evidence against, the causal realist and anti-realist interpretations. The explanation for this seemingly contradictory appearance, I argue, is that Hume in fact maintains a position that is intermediate between realism and anti-realism as just defined. According to my interpretation, Hume traces the impression of necessary connection or power between causes and effects to a feeling in the mind, and thereby denies that our discourse about causes implicates the existence of powers or forces linking causes to effects. At the same time, however, he recognizes causal judgments as genuine propositions, susceptible to truth and falsehood, that are not simply equivalent to statements of regularities in nature. Hence, anti-realist interpretations are right to emphasize that Hume rejects an account of causation in terms of powers or necessary connections, but wrong to suppose that this leads him either to reductionism or emotivism. Causal realist interpretations are right to suppose that Hume attributes a non-reductionistic truth-value to causal statements, but wrong to think that the truth or falsity of these statements results from correspondence with powers or forces.

To explain this interpretation, I begin by linking the standard of equality in Hume's discussion of space and time to his aesthetic and moral theories (see Chapter 5.4). As we saw in Chapter 5.4, a standard of equality is a natural product of the mind in geometry and so, too, he thinks a standard of taste is a natural step for the mind to make when making aesthetic judgments, evidenced in his essay, 'Of the Standard of Taste'. The problem that occupies Hume in this essay is introduced by the following simple observation: There is a great variety of taste in the world and the sentiments of people with regard to beauty and deformity differ. This may lead one to scepticism as to whether anything is ever really beautiful or ugly. One might, for example, think that there is no such thing as beauty or deformity, in which case seeking the real beauty or deformity would be a wasted effort (EMPL 230). Alternatively, one might think that there is an abundance of truths about beauty and deformity. This is because what is beautiful depends on the particular person at hand, so it is true for that particular person, and so on, such that there is no such thing as a right or wrong response to a work of art, in which case again seeking the real beauty or deformity would be a wasted effort. Hume is concerned to refute this rather seductive view in his essay by finding a way to settle disputes about taste.

He argues that a standard of taste is not only a natural step for the mind to make, but is also a *necessary* step in order to make decisive judgments in aesthetics, that is, to approve of one sentiment of taste and disapprove of another. He says that 'It is natural for us to seek a *Standard of Taste*. . .by which the various sentiments of men may be reconciled; at least, a decision afforded, confirming one sentiment, and condemning another' (EMPL 229). He thinks that commonsense dictates that the taste of all people is not on equal footing and that some sentiments of taste will be thought of as preferable to others:

> Whoever would assert an equality of genius and elegance between OGILBY and MILTON, or BUNYAN and ADDISON, would be thought to defend no less an extravagance, than if he

had maintained. . .[that] a pond [is] as extensive as the ocean. Though there may be found persons, who give preference to the former authors; no one pays attention to such a taste; and we pronounce without scruple the sentiment of these pretended critics to be absurd and ridiculous (EMPL 230–231).

He aims to show that while it is 'certain, that beauty and deformity. . .are not qualities in objects, but belong entirely to the sentiment' (EMPL 229; EHU 12.3.33; SBN 165), it is nevertheless possible and appropriate to determine on this basis 'a true and perfect standard of taste' (EMPL 234). This standard can then be used to adjudicate between different sentiments. The true and perfect standard is what Hume attempts to reveal thus, and he must do so by somehow balancing both views that judgments of taste are based on sentiment, and that there are correct aesthetic judgments.

Generating a perfect standard of taste involves correcting our aesthetic sentiments by reflecting on the general rules of art, which have yet to be systematized (EMPL 236). These rules are founded on experience and on the observation 'of the common sentiments of human nature', namely, 'what has been universally found to please in all countries and in all ages' (EMPL 231–2, 235). Hume points to the fact that some works of art attain critical approval across the barriers of culture and time, as when ancient authors such as Homer and Cicero charm modern readers. He suggests that such a convergence of taste identifies a work of real genius. An examination of these works of genius should provide us with rules of composition for good art. Consequently, we must study human nature, society, and history to see how and why this piece of art is suited to please or displease the human frame, as 'it must be allowed that there are certain qualities in objects, which are fitted by nature to produce those particular feelings' (EMPL 235). Once we have established these general rules of art, we can use them to infer that lesser degrees of the same qualities please or displease a sufficiently refined and practiced art critic.

Discovering the relationship that nature has placed between 'the form and the sentiment' is not an easy task, so Hume specifies that certain favorable circumstances need to be present when one makes a judgment in matters of artistic taste (EMPL 232). For instance, one needs a serene mind, a recollection of thought, and due attention to the object. A sound state of the organ is also required: a person with a fever is not a good judge in a decision concerning flavors, nor is a person with jaundice fit to give a verdict about colors (EMPL 232–3).

In addition, one needs a delicate imagination. Indeed, it could even be said that the delicate imagination is at the root of being a good judge. In order to define this delicacy, he offers the story of Sancho's kinsmen. The kinsmen were asked to give their judgment on wine which was supposed to be of excellent quality. One pronounces it good except for a small taste of leather and the other one pronounces it good, except for a small taste of iron. Both men were heartily ridiculed for their judgments until the hogshead was emptied and an old key with a leathern thong attached was discovered at the bottom. It is being sensitive to these types of properties that is the root of being a good judge. One has a delicacy of taste when one's organs are so fine that nothing escapes them and at the same time so exact as to perceive every ingredient in the composition (EMPL 235). This delicacy is improved by frequent practice and by making numerous comparisons between types and degrees of artistic excellence. Those critics with adequate experience of a particular art form will perceive cases with greater accuracy resulting in a more reflective decision of the whole experience. Frequent practice and comparison will also direct the imagination to expect various combinations of properties in light of one's recognition that it is a thing of a specific kind. Practice and comparison thus heightens the subject's awareness of disruptive impressions (the taste of iron or leather), or missing impressions. In sum, practice and comparison improves taste.

The mind must also be free from prejudice, as prejudice destroys sound judgment. In order to check the influence of prejudice, one is required to have good sense. Part of having good sense will involve being able to judge how suited something is for serving its purpose, as 'Every work of art has also a certain end or purpose for which it is calculated; and is deemed more or less perfect, as it is more or less fitted to attain this end' (EMPL 240). Poetry, for example, is intended to provide pleasure by exciting the passions and the imagination, the point of history is to educate, and so on. The verdict of those critics who have developed all these qualities affords the ultimate standard of taste. Given these strict requirements on the delicacy of taste, Hume's standard requires a considerably refined taste. He admits there are few people who are qualified to give judgment on a work of art; nevertheless, he thinks that such people are easily discernible in society (EMPL 241, 243). Those works of art that are approved by practiced, intelligent, and impartial judges with delicate taste over a long period of time are works of merit.[43]

Hume acknowledges while most disagreements can be resolved by appeal to the judge, there a couple of unresolvable aesthetic disagreements. First, there are natural differences in persons' basic disposition of character that make some prefer horror movies, while others prefer musical comedies (EMPL 243–4). The second complicating circumstance is the particular manners and opinions of the age one lives in. The good critic must attempt to overcome the challenge of cultural prejudice (EMPL 243–5). He writes of his own work that also, 'A critic of a different age or nation, who should peruse this discourse, must have all these circumstances in his eye, and must place himself in the same situation as the audience, in order to form a true judgment of the oration' (EMPL 239).

At this point, it is important to clearly distinguish between the rules and standards on Hume's account. The general rules of art are established principles based on observation and experience, particularly, the tendencies of certain things to give human beings pleasure or displeasure over a long period of time. These rules then serve as directives to guide critical reflection on aesthetic sentiments. The 'true and perfect' standard, however, is produced in the imagination of the delicate art critic on the other hand. This standard is generated by things like practice and comparison, and importantly, by reflecting on the general rules of art. The rules assist in the producing the ideal standard in the imagination of the delicate critic. Note that rules and standards are produced differently. The rules, although based on human sentiments, are in a sense determined independently of the delicacy of the art critic because the rules are empirical generalizations based on what has universally found to please or displease us in all countries and ages. The ideal standard, however, is produced directly in the imagination of the delicate art critic.

It is thus the perfect standard produced in the imagination that establishes that one particular aesthetic judgment is better than another, rather than the application of the general rules of art alone. After all, one can misunderstand and/or misapply the general rules of art; Hume was well aware that people vary greatly in reasoning abilities. In a long footnote on the reason of animals at *Enquiry*,

Hume offers many examples of the differences in human under-standing. Some people are better at carrying on 'chain of conse-quences to a greater length than another'; some are better at seeing the 'bigger picture' so to speak; others are able to think for longer without running into confusion; others are more apt to allow preju-dice or emotion have an effect on their reasoning, and so on (EHU 9.5n20; SBN 107n). Thus, Hume specifies that the practiced art critic needs good sense, a serene mind, sound state of the organ, a delicate imagination, in order to understand and apply the rules appropri-ately. The standard produced in the mind of such an art critic affords a decision between conflicting judgments of taste, and not the sole application of the rules themselves.

Even though the rules of art have never been formally laid out, appealing to the rules, however, can show why a delicate art critic applauds or condemns a particular piece of artwork. Hume says that producing these general rules of art is like finding the key with the leathern thong, which justified the judgment of Sancho's kinsmen. This means that the rules can be used in the same way that the dis-covery of the key was used. If the delicate art critic claims that a par-ticular artwork, poem or song is elegant, the claim can be confirmed by pointing out the rule that identifies the particular elegance of the piece of art, poem, or song. In order to silence the bad critic, one can point to the general principles of art and the bad critic must be forced to conclude that the fault lies within him or herself and that they themselves lack this delicacy by which every beauty and defor-mity may be found in any composition (EMPL 235f.). The rules thus can provide a way of showing why one's taste is better than another's, although the good taste of the delicate art critic remains superior whether it is confirmed by the rules or not. Where we can find them, rules of this sort are useful for separating true from pretend critics, if only in allowing us to point out inconsistencies in critical response.

There are evident parallels between the explanation of a standard of equality outlined in the first book of the *Treatise* and the 'Of the Standard of Taste'. The standards described in both cases are natural in that it is a product of our need to judge, whether it is to do with equality or beauty and deformity. The standard, which is also arrived at through review and correction by rules based on expe-rience, is also something within the mind's power to assemble that will enable one to compare judgments about lines, or tastes and choose between them. The existence of this standard in Hume's system is then essential because it allows us to confirm one sentiment of taste or equality and condemn another.[44] The standard thus is a 'certain criterion' that is set up as an ideal that can be applied to secure a judgment on the matter (EMPL 242). When the question arises as to which piece of art is the more beautiful, the standard for judgment depends on the delicate imagination of the practiced art critic. With increasing delicacy, therefore, art critics make comparisons between types and degrees of artistic excellence, and this activity results in an imaginative projection of a perfect standard that enables them to judge real beauty or deformity of artworks.

Hume thinks that moral qualities such as virtue and vice, just like the aesthetic qualities of beauty and deformity, belong to feeling, and do not represent anything in the object.[45] He claims for instance that the 'approbation of moral qualities. . .proceeds entirely from a moral taste, and from certain sentiments of pleasure or disgust, which arise upon the contemplation and view of particular qualities of characters' (THN 3.3.1.15; SBN 581). Moreover, he emphasizes many times that one must account for the correcting of moral sentiments by reflection. In order to arrive at an established judgment in morals, we must overlook our present situation and fix on '*steady* and *general* points of view', just like we do in the case of beauty (THN 3.3.1.15; SBN 582). A beautiful painting seen at a distance is less striking than when it is seen much closer, but we do not say that the painting is less beautiful because of that, since 'we know what effect it will have in such a position, and by that reflection we correct its momentary appearance' (THN 3.3.1.16; SBN 582).[46] In morals, we must be careful to correct and adjust our sentiments by reflection. This is especially pertinent when assigning praise and blame, as our sentiments tend to differ depending on 'the present disposition of the mind' (THN SBN 582), and how near or far we are from the particular situation. It may be that our diligent and faithful servant will 'excite stronger sentiments of love and kindness' in us than a distant historical figure such as Marcus Brutus, but that does not mean that we think that the former character is more admirable than the latter (THN 3.3.1.16; SBN 582). 'The tendencies of actions and characters, not their real accidental consequences, are alone regarded in our moral determinations' (EPM 5.41n; SBN 228n). He argues also that we should make allowances for a certain amount of selfishness in our dealings with people, because we know that it is just part of human nature; he says: 'By this reflexion we correct those sentiments of blame' (THN 3.3.1.17; SBN 583). Moreover, just as artistic delicacy is improved by frequent comparison, so too by comparison, 'we fix the epithets of praise or blame, and learn how to assign the due degrees of each' (EMPL 238).

These sorts of corrections by reflection are said to be common in regard to all the senses. For instance, the deceptive evidence provided by the senses such as the crooked appearance of the oar in the water or the double image which is produced by pressing the eyeball, can be corrected with the use of reason (EHU 12.1.6; SBN 151). Distinguishing between the fictions of poetry and genuine belief also involves thinking about general rules (THN 1.3.10.11–2; SBN 631–2). He compares the process to the correcting of the senses, ''Tis thus the understanding corrects the appearances of the senses, and makes us imagine, that an object at twenty foot distance seems even to the eye as large as one of the same dimensions at ten' (THN 1.3.10.11–2; SBN 631–2). The process of correcting our sensory perceptions by reflection is compared to that of correcting our moral sentiments also in Book III of the *Treatise*. Just as our sentiments of praise and blame can vary depending on how near or far we are from the situation, so too can our feelings of sympathy.

> All objects seem to diminish by the distance, but tho' the appearance of objects to our senses be the original standard, by which we judge of them, yet we do not say, that they actually diminish by the distance; but correcting the appearance by reflexion, arrive at a more constant and establish'd judgment concerning them. In a like manner, tho' sympathy be much fainter than our concern for ourselves, and a sympathy with persons remote from us much fainter than that with persons near and contiguous; yet we neglect all these differences in our calm judgments concerning the characters of men (THN 3.3.3.2; SBN 603).

He notes that it is common for us to change our situation in this way: we meet people everyday who are in different situations than ourselves, and we would not be able to talk to them if we stayed constantly in that situation and point of view which is particular to us. A common point of view is needed to reach agreement about things amongst humans (THN 3.3.1.30; SBN 591; EPM 9.2; SBN 272). Indeed, without such corrections to our sentiments we would never to be able to 'think or talk steadily on any subject' (EPM 5.41; SBN 229). Hume goes on to say that this process of correcting of our moral sentiments through reflection coupled with the daily intercourse of sentiments in society and conversation, makes us to form some 'general *inalterable standard*' (THN 3.3.3.2; SBN 603, my emphasis; see also EPM 5.42; SBN 229).[47] This fixed standard enables us to 'approve or disapprove of characters and manners' (THN 3.3.3.2; SBN 603). The standard then is necessary in Hume's moral theory, just as it is in his aesthetic theory, to secure a judgment.

Hume emphasizes in his moral theory that our feelings will not always correspond to the determinations made by judgment; indeed, sometimes our feelings can be very 'stubborn' (THN 3.3.1.16; SBN 582), ''Tis seldom men heartily love what lies at a distance from them, and what no way redounds to their particular benefit' (THN 3.3.1.18; SBN 583). In 'Of the Standard of Taste', also, he argues that not everyone's feelings will match up to the judgments made by the understanding. This is because certain favorable circumstances need to be present when judging, such as a serene mind, due attention to the object, a delicate imagination and so on, in order to 'make them play with facility and exactness, according to their general and established principles' (EMPL 232). When any of these circumstances are absent, one will be unable to judge that 'universal beauty' (EMPL 232–3). However, while our sentiments and passions cannot be corrected directly by reflection, experience teaches that we are at the very least able to correct our language and this is enough to suit everyday purposes (THN 3.3.1.16; SBN 582). Hume points this out on at least three occasions. He states that the 'passions do not always follow our corrections; but these corrections serve sufficiently to regulate our abstract notions, and are alone regarded, when we pronounce in general concerning the degrees of vice and virtue' (THN 3.3.1.21; SBN 585), and that, 'And tho' the *heart* does not always take part with those general notions, or regulate its love and hatred by them, yet are they sufficient for discourse, and serve all our purposes in company, in the pulpit, on the theatre, and in the schools' (THN 3.3.3.2; SBN 603; EPM 5.42; SBN 229). Even though our sentiments and passions might change slowly in contrast to the determinations made by judgment, the process of adjusting our sentiments by the use of rules can nonetheless alter our abstract ideas, and we can correct our usage of general terms in language accordingly to align with the determinations of judgment.

Making judgments in aesthetics and morals is not only a product of review, reflection and discussion, but also presupposes the presence and application of general terms, such as beauty, deformity, virtue, vice, and so on, in our language. In the case of morals: he says that language must 'invent a peculiar set of terms in order to express those universal sentiments of censure or approbation which arise from humanity' (EPM 9.8; SBN 274). In 'Of the Standard of Taste', he notes that despite the obvious fact that there is a wide variety in judgments of taste in the world, there does appear on the surface to be agreement amongst people over the evaluative force of general terms:

> There are certain terms in every language, which import blame, and others praise; and all men, who use the same tongue, must agree in their application of them. Every voice is united in applauding elegance, propriety, simplicity and spirit in writing; and in blaming faustian, affectation, coldness, and a false brilliancy (EMPL 227).

On the level of surface discourse, it looks like we agree on a good deal because we regularly use generic terms like 'beauty' and 'deformity' that carry with them positive or negative associations. We all agree that if something is beautiful then it is to be admired or applauded and that if something is ugly, it should be condemned. The general agreement, however, completely disappears when critics come to particulars because there is a wide divergence over the meaning of central terms.[48] Moral and aesthetic judgments reveal great disagreement once you plunge below the surface of language. When you look closer at how people apply the terms like beauty and deformity or virtue and vice, you realize that people actually apply the terms in all sorts of incompatible ways.

There are four main parallels between Hume's causal, aesthetic and moral theories. First, we have had the occasion to observe that when we ascribe necessity to causal relations, we ascribe to objects qualities that exist only in the mind and not in the object. Second, just as our aesthetic and moral discourse contains general terms, so too does our causal discourse. Since the idea of necessary connection is a general term, it follows that for Hume that it is an abstract idea.

Forming the abstract idea of a necessary connection between cause and effect is a consequence of observing regular events (THN 1.3.14.20; SBN 164). Certain causes and effects strike us as regular in everyday life and we tend to respond to observed conjunctions with an automatic expectation of the latter's being repeated. To help navigate the world, we seek, naturally enough, a way of referring to our experiences of these regularities. Not only do we need a vocabulary to express our confidences about necessary causal connections to others in everyday living, but also to express our doubts when other causes and effects are not so regular. In conversation then, we work out what we believe about what we believe causes what. The strength of the expectation and the degrees of belief formed correspond to things like the amount of feeling we have and the frequency and vividness of the observations ('there are habits with various degrees of force proportion'd to the inferior degrees of steadiness and uniformity in our conduct', THN 1.2.12.4–6; SBN 131–3). We observe, we expect, and, prompted by our expectations, we formulate judgments to the effect that this and that event are necessarily connected and make predictions on that basis. Expressions of attitudes concerning causal connections have been gained thus on the basis of empirical experience gathered over longer periods of time, not to mention through conversational exchanges with other individuals.

This brings us to the third parallel between causes, morals, and aesthetics: general rules. General rules provide corrective guidelines for the evaluation of those feelings which form the basis of causal, moral, and aesthetic judgments. As we observed in Chapter 6.6, Hume supplements his account of causation by offering eight rules to help us determine when objects really do lie in the relation of cause and effect (THN 1.3.15; SBN 175). He thinks that in order to fix the just standard of causes, we need to frequently review and correct our causal judgments by reflection on general rules (THN 1.4.1.5; SBN 182). In fact, Hume insists twice that we always 'ought to regulate our judgment concerning causes and effects' by these rules (THN 1.3.13.11; SBN; 1.4.1.5; SBN 182). In fact, he claims that these rules are the only 'logic' used in his reasoning and, he does use them consistently throughout all three books of the *Treatise* (THN 1.3.15.11; SBN 175).

After spending some time correcting our judgments about causes via the rules, surely it is a natural step for the imagination to then form an ideal standard of a necessary connection between cause and effect. The standard can then be used as a decisive criterion to judge between differing causal sentiments. This true and decisive standard for judging whether a particular cause and effect pair is truly necessarily connected will no doubt depend on the delicacy of the practiced causalist. The practiced causalist is a person who has frequently reviewed and corrected his or her causal judgments, as it is necessary that distinctions be made, experiments conducted, comparisons formed, and conclusions drawn in order to achieve a discerning judgment about a necessary connection between cause and effect.

The practiced causalist will no doubt need a delicate imagination, not to mention keen observation and concentration skills, are needed when applying the rules. This is because one must 'carefully separate whatever is superfluous, and enquire by new experiments' to make sure that every particular circumstance of the first experiment is essential to it (THN 1.3.15.11; SBN 175). We then subject the new experiment to that same scrutiny, taking care to conduct our investigation with the highest 'constancy' and 'sagacity' (THN 1.3.15.11; SBN 175). Additionally, Hume specifies that the inquirer conducting these experiments has persistence, caution, and good sense because the surrounding circumstances can be very complex and might even escape 'our strictest attention'. Even so, it is very important to engage in repeated experiments to separate what is superfluous in causal relations. A delicate imagination is thus needed so as to perceive every single component in experiments about causes, without allowing any element to be overlooked.[49] When we want to know whether a cause and effect are truly necessarily connected, we turn to the delicate imagination of the practiced causalist. The delicate imagination of the practiced causalist provides a fixed standard for judging between differing causal sentiments. Any causal judgment which corresponds to, agrees with, or is in conformity with the standard is true and conversely, any causal judgment which diverges from the standard is false.

There is one final parallel between Hume's causal, aesthetic, and moral theories. In the causal case also, we should not expect our feelings to always correspond with the determinations of judgment. Consider Hume's example of the unfortunate man who is hung out from a high tower in a cage of iron, and cannot stop trembling when he surveys the ground below. By reflection, the man knows that he is perfectly secure from falling, 'by his experience of the solidity of the iron, which supports him'; however, the man's feelings of fear are not appeased by this reflection: '[t]he circumstances of depth and descent strike so strongly upon him, that their influence cannot be destroyed by the contrary circumstances of solidity and support, which ought to give him perfect security. His imagination runs away with its object, and excites a passion proportion'd to it' (THN 1.3.13.10; SBN 148–9). Not only might not our feelings correspond to our judgments, in some cases a correct causal judgment might be produced without a feeling at all. In his account of belief, Hume notes that experience may even operate on our minds in a manner that is entirely unnoticed by us. This is the case 'in all the most established and uniform conjunctions of causes and effects, such as those of gravity, impulse, solidity, etc., the mind never carries its view expressly to consider any past experience' (THN 1.3.8.13–4; SBN 104).[50] He goes on to say that a belief about a causal relation may be produced without the influence of custom at all; Hume notes that 'we may attain the knowledge of a particular cause merely by one experiment, provided it be made with judgment, and after a careful removal of all foreign and superfluous circumstances' (THN 1.3.8.14; SBN 105). Thus, a single, properly conducted experiment under the best conditions may allow the mind to 'build an argument', and 'What we have found once to follow from any object, we conclude will for ever follow from it' (THN 1.3.12.3; SBN 131).

Since a habit cannot be acquired through one instance, it may be thought that the resulting belief might not be the effect of custom after all. Hume's response is elegant. The difficulty is removed, he says, when we remember that we have had many million experiences to convince us of the uniformity principle '*that like objects, plac'd in like circumstances, will always produce like effect*'. So although the connection of ideas is not habitual after one experiment, the connection is comprehended under another principle that is habitual, and consequently 'in all cases, we transfer our experience to instances of which we have no experience, either *expressly* or *tacitly*, either *directly* or *indirectly*' (THN 1.3.8.14; SBN 105).

7.5. SUMMARY

This chapter surveyed Hume's account of necessity and its application to the free will debate. Finally, I defended an interpretation of the necessary connection according to which Hume thinks that statements about causes are based on psychological mechanisms developed in response to the experience of regularities and not on powers existing in objects. Hume also suggests that by consistently using reflective principles to correct causal judgments we may arrive at a decisive standard by which to judge causes and effects as being necessarily connected. The imaginary standard establishes when one can be said to make a true judgment, and when one can appropriately use the relevant general terms in discourse.

NOTES

1 See Mackie (1974: 3) and Sosa and Tooley (1993: 31).
2 For more detail on the terms realism and anti-realism and their application to causality, see Coventry (2006: chapter 2).
3 For more on Hume's critique of Locke's theory of causal power, and other similarities and differences between their theories, see Coventry (2003).
4 THN 1.3.14.10; SBN 160; EHU 7.1.24; SBN 70.
5 EHU 7.1.20; SBN 66; THN 1.3.14.12; SBN 632.
6 See also THN 1.3.14.27; SBN 168; EPM App. 1.21; SBN 294: 'we transfer the determination of the thought to external objects, and suppose any real intelligible connexion betwixt them; that being a quality, which can only belong to the mind that considers them'.
7 See also the 1751 letter to Gilbert Elliot of Minto, 'We feel, after the constant conjunction, an easy Transition from one Idea to the other, or a Connexion in the Imagination. And as it is usual for us to transfer our own Feelings to the Objects on which they are dependent, we attach the internal Sentiment to the external Objects', in Grieg (1932: I, 155–6).
8 These definitions have caused much controversy; see Garrett (1997: chapter 5) for a thorough discussion of the two definitions and their reception in the literature.
9 There is a parallel here to Hume's definitions of virtue; for more detail see Garrett (1997: 107f.).
10 For a detailed account of Hume on moral responsibility, see Russell (1995).
11 Russell (1995: 64).
12 This summation in this paragraph is taken largely from Russell (1995: 64).
13 Leibniz (1989: 37–9).
14 The ensuing discussion in this section is taken from Coventry (2006: chapter 5).
15 For other varieties of realist interpretations, see Costa (1989: 172–90); Broughton (1987: 13, 217–44); Broughton (1983: 3–18). See also

Livingston (1984); Craig (1987); and Craig, 'Hume on Causality; Projectivist *and* Realist?' in Reid and Richman (2000: 113–21), for a slightly different interpretation.

16 See Wright (1983: 129).
17 Wright, 'Hume's Causal Realism: Recovering a Traditional Interpretation', in Reid and Richman (2000: 35, 40, 42, 44–45).
18 Wright (1983: 156).
19 Wright (1983: 161). See also Wright's 'Hume's Causal Realism: Recovering a Traditional Interpretation', in Reid and Richman (2000: 34–5, 39).
20 Wright, 'Hume's Causal Realism: Recovering a Traditional Interpretation', in Reid and Richman (2000: sections 2 and 3).
21 Strawson (1989: 3). See also his most recent article, 'David Hume: Objects and Power', in Reid and Richman (2000: 31–51).
22 Strawson (1989: 147).
23 Strawson (1989: 12).
24 Strawson (1989: 2f.).
25 See Strawson's 'David Hume: Objects and Power', in Reid and Richman (2000: 37).
26 See Craig (1987: 124), and Strawson (1987: chapter 12), and Wright's 'Hume's Causal Realism', in Reid and Richman (2000: 89).
27 See Wright's 'Hume's Causal Realism', in Reid and Richman (2000: 48).
28 For further elaboration on these and other arguments in favor of realist interpretations, see Strawson (1989: sections 14–20), and his contribution to *The New Hume Debate* in Reid and Richman (2000: 31–51). See also Wright (1983: 129), and his contribution to *The New Hume Debate* in Reid and Richman (2000: 172–90), and Broughton (1987: 217–44).
29 For further detail on these arguments and others, see contributions by Blackburn, Winkler, Bell, Flage, and Jacobson in Reid and Richman (2000).
30 See also EHU 7.2.28; SBN 75 and THN 2.3.2.4; SBN 409.
31 In Leland (1757), *A View of the Principal Deistical Writers*. Taken from Fieser (ed.) (2000: 142, 147).
32 In Taylor, 'Causation', in Edwards (1967: 58, 60); see also Taylor (1963: 287–313, [291]).
33 In Basson (1958: 73–6).
34 Mach (1960: 580).
35 Reid (2001: 3–12, 3, 6, 12).
36 Other commentators who hold this view also includes Mackie (1974: 198f.) and Phalen (1977: 17, 43–57, [53]). See also Robinson, 'Hume's Two Definitions of a "Cause"', reprinted in Chappell (1966: 138f.); Woolhouse (1988: 149–50); Penelhum (1975: 46, 53–7); Capaldi (1975: 120–3); Tooley, 'Causation: Reductionism Versus Realism', in Sosa and Tooley (1993: 172); Bennett (1971); Jacobson (1989: 325–38, [336n6]); Greenberg (1955: 612–23, [613]); and Prichard (1950: 188).
37 THN 1.3.2.11; SBN 77; EHU 7.2.27; SBN 75.
38 In Home (1758; 226).

39 Stroud, ' "Gilding or Staining" the World with "Sentiments" and "Phantasms" ', in Reid and Richman (2000: 26). See also Stroud (1977: 86) and Pears (1990: chapter 7).

40 Stroud writes that 'At the most, the projectivist account of causation produces: "a kind of confusion or nonsense on our part, perhaps with an accompanying illusion of having coherent thoughts of that kind when we really do not". . .[W]e could not intelligibly think that necessity. . .is a feature of the relation between two external objects or events, that the two are necessarily connected', in Reid and Richman (2000: 23–4).

41 Forbes argues that, 'Hume's view is that we. . .make a mistake: we project something essentially "inner" onto the external world, and come to the mistaken belief that the concept of necessity we have applies to propositions in virtue of the objective properties of ideas, and, as a consequence of this, we mistakenly believe that modal judgements can be true or false', in Forbes (1985: 218).

42 See EHU 7.2.28; SBN 75; EHU 8.1.5; SBN 82; THN 1.3.8.12; SBN 103; THN 1.3.14.24; SBN 166; THN 1.3.14.27; SBN 168; THN 2.3.2.4; SBN 400; THN 2.3.1.4; SBN 409 and AB 34; SBN 660.

43 I owe this way of putting the point in this final sentence to Garrett (2003: 108, 161–79, [173]).

44 Consider also Hume's claim that in dealing with property, the need for a standard is to decide disputes. No certain standard exists: one cannot distinguish impossibility from improbability from probability in cases of disputed possession. Nevertheless, one needs to, 'Mark the precise limits of the one and the other, and shew the standard by which we may decide all disputes that may arise, and, as we find by experience, frequently do arise upon this subject' (THN 3.2.3.7; SBN 506).

45 THN 3.1.2; SBN 470f.; EPM App.1.12; SBN 291; EHU 12.3.33; SBN 165.

46 Hume compares the moral case to the aesthetic case also at EPM App.1.13; SBN 291.

47 Hume has much more to say about rules in his moral theory also: there are also the rules of justice and the rules of good breeding. For a thorough discussion of rules in his moral theory, see Hearn (1970: section IV).

48 Hume also distinguishes another type of divergence of the sort we are all familiar with. For example, within our own social circles, one might notice a difference in taste or morals with your friend's, even when you have grown up in exactly the same culture as that person, and without our own social circles (i.e., cultural differences) (EPML 226–7).

49 Given that 'the imagination. . .[is] the ultimate judge of all systems of philosophy', 'a vigorous and strong imagination is of all talents the most proper to procure belief' (THN 1.4.4.1; SBN 225). However, he warns that 'a lively imagination very often degenerates into madness or folly. . .When the imagination. . .acquires such a vivacity as disorders all its powers and faculties, there is no means of distinguishing betwixt truth and falsehood' (THN 1.3.10.9; SBN 123).

50 See also THN 1.3.12.7; SBN 133. The fact that experience may produce a belief and a judgment about causes and effects without being once thought of explains why we are so convinced of the uniformity principle, THN 1.3.8.13–4; SBN 103–4.

CHAPTER 8

SCEPTICISM

Hume's philosophy has traditionally been thought of as extremely sceptical. After all, he calls himself a 'sceptic' at the end of Book 1 of *A Treatise of Human Nature* and characterizes his philosophy as 'very sceptical' in the Abstract to the *Treatise* (AB 27; SBN 657). Much debate remains, however, as to what his scepticism amounts to and how his scepticism is related to other more positive parts of his philosophical project. In fact, balancing Hume's scepticism with his constructive enterprise of establishing a science of human nature is said to be the central task facing every Hume scholar. Some commentators think Hume's scepticism ultimately destroys any positive attempt at the science of human nature,[1] while other commentators argue that his scepticism supports or is in harmony with his science of human nature.[2] This chapter examines Hume's presentation of a number of sceptical arguments at *Treatise* 1.4. First, he tackles scepticism about the operations of reason (8.1), then theories about the external world, that is, matter (8.2–4), and theories to do with the internal world, that is, mind (8.5–8.6), and, finally, the effects of scepticism on the practice of philosophy (8.7). The chapter ends by considering the role of scepticism in his science of human nature in favor of the position that scepticism is an integral element backing up Hume's philosophical program.

8.1. SCEPTICISM ABOUT REASON

One of Hume's most notorious sceptical moments occurs at *Treatise* 1.4.1. Here, he offers an argument purporting to show that 'all is uncertain, and that our judgment is not in any thing possest of any measures of truth and falshood' (THN 1.4.1.7; SBN 183).

He seemed to think the sceptical arguments to do with reason were important as he referred to it at least three times, twice before the argument occurs and once after;[3] in addition, the argument shows up in Philo and Cleanthes' discussion of scepticism in the very first part of the mature *Dialogues Concerning Natural Religion* (DNR 8).

The sceptical argument about reason has two main parts.[4] The first part concludes that, 'all knowledge degenerates into probability' (THN 1.4.1.1; SBN 180). Even though the rules are 'certain and infallible' in the demonstrative sciences, those of us who apply the rules have 'fallible and uncertain faculties', and mistakes are often made (THN 1.4.1.1; SBN 180). We must then form a second judgment about whether we have performed any given demonstration correctly, and this second judgment is only probable. In the case of mathematics, we double-check our proofs, confirm with our peers, and so on. The addition of 'new probabilities' produces a greater degree of force in the habit and leads to a gradual increase in assurance and what accounts for the increase is constant conjunction, 'the constant union of causes and effects according to past experience and observation' (THN 1.4.1.2; SBN 180–1).

The second part of the argument is that the force of any probability judgment will be diminished until it is reduced to nothing by successive applications of a similar process of reasoning. For in every probability judgment, we ought to correct our first judgment, 'deriv'd from the nature of the object, by another judgment, deriv'd from the nature of the understanding' (THN 1.4.1.5; SBN 182). Even a person with loads of good sense and experience is susceptible to all sorts of errors. This provides a new standard of probability to correct the first one. Further, similar concerns about our fallible and uncertain faculties and their liability to error require us to subject this second judgment to a 'doubt deriv'd from the possibility of error in the estimation we make of the truth and fidelity of our faculties' (THN 1.4.1.6; SBN 182). This new judgment, even if it is favorable to the judgment we made about understanding, still increases the initial doubt and so weakens our first evidence (THN 1.4.1.6; SBN 182). This requires us to adjust the first probability downward, even if experience shows that we are quite good in forming this kind of judgment. Hume seems to have held the view that when two uncertainties are compounded, no matter what they are, the result is even greater uncertainty. Then, the initial evaluation of one's competence must itself be evaluated, which further reduces the original probability. The process continues *ad infinitum*, but because the initial probability is a finite object, it must eventually perish under the infinite decrease. So, since we have to perform infinitely many assessments, each diminishes the initial probability judgment to some degree, there is eventually, as Hume puts it, 'a total extinction of belief and evidence' (THN 1.4.1.6; SBN 183) and we are left with a mere idea, with none of the force and vivacity that characterizes a belief.[5]

Does Hume assent to this argument, making him a sceptic, who holds that 'all is uncertain, and that our judgment is not in any thing possest of any measures of truth and falshood' (THN 1.4.1.7; SBN 183)? No. Hume thinks that no one can be a total sceptic. A total sceptic is one who believes nothing. Since belief influences behavior, a total sceptic is one who would never act. Nature forces us to act, so there can be no such thing as a total sceptic. An extinction of belief does not take place as nature has determined us to judge as well as to breathe and feel (THN 1.4.1.7; SBN 183). The real question Hume thinks is not how to refute this sort of sceptical argument, but to explain instead how it happens that we continue to believe in the face of such arguments. In fact, his own theory is perfectly suited to such an explanation; he even claims that the point of putting forward the sceptical argument is to confirm his account of belief as an act of the sensitive part of our nature. The fact that beliefs cannot be destroyed by 'mere ideas and reflections' shows that belief is not an act of reason but rather consists in 'some sensation or peculiar manner of conception' (THN 1.4.1.8; SBN 184). If belief were a simple act of thought, then it would destroy itself and terminate in a complete suspense of judgment.

Hume recognizes that the sceptical argument can be applied to his own account of belief as well (THN 1.4.1.9; SBN 185). His response is that we retain a degree of belief sufficient for our purposes because we lack the mental capacity to pursue our reflections in this manner:[6] the mental strain of the examination stops a complete loss of belief from occurring. In sum, the sceptical argument seems to be that reason considered alone undermines itself, reason 'furnishes invincible arguments against itself' and would actually result in a loss of belief, or 'conviction or assurance', in any subject were it not for the fact that the sceptical reasoning is too complicated for us (DNR 8).

8.2. THE EXISTENCE OF EXTERNAL OBJECTS

Hume's elaborate psychological explanation of how human nature leads us to believe that our perceptions represent continuously existing objects that are independent of the mind is notoriously murky. The question he takes up is: 'What causes our belief in the existence of bodies?' which is then split into two closely related questions:

(a) Why do we attribute continued existence to bodies?
(b) Why do we attribute a mind-independent existence to them?

The first question concerns why we believe that external bodies exist when not present to the senses, why we suppose that external objects continue to exist in the same manner even when we are not looking at them. The second question concerns why we believe that objects are independent of the mind and exist without our perceiving them, that is, why we believe that bodies exist independently and externally from the mind and to the senses. These two questions imply each other. It should be emphasized at the outset that these beliefs cannot be challenged. Hume thinks that nature forces us to accept these beliefs; we are forced to believe in the existence of an external world.[7] The question is not *do* we have these beliefs in continued and distinct existences but *why* do we have those beliefs? There are three possible sources for these beliefs in continued and distinct existence: the senses, reason and the imagination. Not surprisingly, it will turn out that neither the senses nor reason can do the job and that the imagination produces the belief in the continued and distinct existence of bodies.

8.2.1. Senses

First, the senses cannot account for continued existence. How can our eyes, for example, assure us that objects continue to exist when the eyes are not operating or are closed? (THN 1.4.2.3; SBN 188) The senses yield impressions, which are perceptions dependent on the mind. A belief arising from the impressions of sense, then, would be an idea of something essentially different from the impressions themselves. We might wish to say that they are images of something distinct from perception, but Hume asks how a single impression could give rise to the belief in a second object, a body distinct from them (THN 1.4.2.4; SBN 189). A second way would be if impressions actually were the distinct bodies. This would require 'a kind of fallacy and illusion' (THN 1.4.2.5; SBN 189). We would have to have an impression of our mind or ourselves and perceptions and see that the two are separate. However, the senses cannot reveal the self: here 'the most profound metaphysics is required' (THN 1.4.2.6; SBN 189). Moreover, deception by the senses seems impossible since the senses present perceptions as they really are (THN 1.4.2.7; SBN 190). Hume was not too concerned with sensory deception. In the *Enquiry*, he considers these sorts of sceptical arguments to do with the senses as 'trite' (EHU 12.1.6; SBN 151). These sorts of arguments only show that the 'senses alone are not implicitly to be depended on', and that they need to be corrected by reason, as well as other 'considerations, derived from the nature of the medium, the distance of the object, and the disposition of the organ' (EHU 12.1.6; SBN 151).

We might believe in external existence because we perceive bodies beyond our human bodies. This is impossible for three reasons. First, we only perceive impressions. Even our body is nothing but a certain collection of impressions (THN 1.4.2.9; SBN 191). Second, secondary qualities such as colors, sounds and smells have no existence in extension. Finally, sight does not reveal distance or 'outness'. The conclusion is that the senses do not give us the idea of the continued existence of bodies. This is confirmed by looking at the three different kinds of impressions conveyed by the senses: in the first class is figure, bulk, motion and solidity, the second class: colors, tastes, sounds, smells and the third class includes pleasures and pains (THN 1.4.2.12; SBN 192). Everyone believes that the third class is dependent on the observer. The vulgar answer the question of a continued and distinct existence by saying that these beliefs are based on the senses and they believe that the first two classes are distinct and continuous in their existence. Philosophers believe that the second class is dependent on the observer. This leaves only the primary qualities as resembling the object. Consequently, the philosophers have asserted that only class one is continuous and distinct in its existence. The vulgar attribute a continued and distinct existence to the very things they feel or see and suppose they can refute the theory from their 'feeling and experience. . .that their very senses contradict this philosophy' (THN 1.4.2.13–4; SBN 192–3). Hume thinks that the distinction between primary and secondary qualities cannot be derived from an analysis of the relevant perceptions, for these perceptions have, as perceptions, exactly the same characteristics. As far as the senses go, 'all perceptions are the same in the manner of their existence' (THN 1.4.2.13; SBN 193).

8.2.2. Reason

Reason is not the cause of these beliefs in continued and distinct existence either, since the arguments that appeal to reasoning are known to the very few and great masses of people manage to produce their beliefs without them (THN 1.4.2.14; SBN 193).[8] The common people believe that everything seen or felt has a continued and distinct existence, so this sentiment must be based on something else, it must proceed from some other faculty apart from the understanding.

The philosophers form a contrary conclusion to the vulgar. The philosophical system is composed of two principles: a distinction between the question of a continued and a distinct existence and a distinction between perceptions and objects. Philosophers recognize that all perceptions are not distinct and dependent upon the mind and that perceptions are interrupted and different at every moment. Consequently, there is no continuous existence of perceptions for the philosophers. On the other hand, the philosophers believe that objects cause our perceptions and that these objects have a continued and distinct existence. In short, philosophers posit a double existence theory by distinguishing between perceptions and objects. It is the object that continues to exist, that is independent of the mind, rather than the perception. This is the system of Descartes and Locke. Hume thought that distinguishing between perceptions and objects is of no real value and that as long as we take the perceptions and objects to be the same, there was no way to reason 'from the existence of one to that of the other' (THN 1.4.2.14; SBN 193). Since the vulgar equate or identify perceptions and objects, the existence of the latter cannot be inferred from the former. If perceptions and objects are confounded, then there is no inference. If there is an inference then we cannot use causal reasoning, which will be shown later. In short, reason cannot justify the theory of double existence so reason cannot be the source of our belief in continued and distinct existence. We are left with the imagination, which gives rise to belief in continued existence in a way that can be explained similar to how belief in causes and effects is explained.

8.2.3. Imagination

There must be some quality of impressions which leads the imagination to produce belief in continued and distinct existence (THN 1.4.2.15; SBN 194). He contends that it is not vivacity, for all impressions have this; and it is not the involuntariness of some impressions, for some pleasures and pains are involuntary and are never considered to exist beyond perception (THN 1.4.2.16; SBN 194). The fact is that some perceptions are more constant and coherent. In the case of the constancy of perceptions, many times we perceive an object, turn our attention away then find perceptions that appear just the same: the 'mountains, and houses, and trees, which lie at present under my eye, have always appear'd to me in the same order' (THN 1.4.2.18; SBN 194). Or his 'bed, table, my books and papers, present themselves in the same manner' and do not change 'upon account of any interruption in [his] seeing or perceiving them' (THN 1.4.2.18; SBN 195). Things do change, however, when we are not observing them so constancy is not the only factor at work. He leaves the room for an hour and finds that the fire is not in the same way as he left it, but he is accustomed in other instances to see a 'like alteration produced in a like time, whether [he] is absent, present, near or remote' (THN 1.4.2.19; SBN 195). The other factor at work is coherence, the fact that these changes occur in an orderly way. Objects, even in their changes, preserve a coherence and have a regular dependence on each other which is the foundation of a kind of reasoning from causation and produces the opinion of their continued existence.

Constancy and coherence affect the imagination differently. Coherence depends on the regularity of operation. Consider this reported chain of events at THN 1.4.2.20; SBN 196:

- 'I hear a noise as of a door turning on its hinges'. If this noise is not from the door, it contradicts all past experience.
- I see a porter moving toward me. If the porter did not come up the stairs, it contradicts all past experience, according to which bodies have gravity and so he did not levitate to the next floor.
- I receive a letter 'from a friend, who says he is two hundred leagues distant'. If the letter did not traverse the sea and was not handed off at various points and travel in different vehicles, it contradicts past experience.

The supposition of continued existence is the only thing that will prevent these contradictions; he finds himself 'naturally led to regard the world, as something real and durable, and as preserving its existence, even when it is no longer present to [his] perception' (THN 1.4.2.20; SBN 197).

The imagination endeavors to preserve the unity of perceptions, and the postulation of continued existence suffices for this purpose. Hume compares this process to the continued motion of a ship (specifically, a galley) after the crew has stopped rowing. This is the same manner as to his view on equality that after correcting many judgments of equality, the imagination, which Hume describes as being 'like a galley', proceeds to invent a 'correct and exact standard of that relation' (THN 1.4.2.22; SBN 198; see Chapter 3.3). The very same principle of the imagination at work with the standard of equality invokes our belief in the 'continu'd existence of body' (THN 1.4.2.22; SBN 198). It is a smooth transition, just as is the inference from effect to cause. The mind observes uniformities and 'naturally continues' until the train is as uniform as possible.

Coherence is not enough to support a system of the continued existence of bodies; constancy is also needed. What happens in our minds is that our perceptions are interrupted, yet constant to a certain degree. It cannot be that the same perception re-occurs after the interruption, but rather an entirely new one. This creates a conflict, 'a kind of contradiction' in our imagination: we want to regard the perception as the same but we must regard it as different (THN 1.4.2.24; SBN 199). To overcome the conflict we 'disguise, as much as possible, the interruption, or rather remove it entirely, by supposing that these interrupted perceptions are connected by a real existence, of which we are insensible' (THN 1.4.2.24; SBN 199). In other words, while our perceptions resemble one another and are at the same time different and interrupted, we avoid the perplexity by creating the fiction of continued existence. Beliefs exist when ideas are made vivid by a process of the imagination. The uniformity of actual perceptions and the regularity of memory reinforce this tendency of the imagination to create a belief, a vivid idea, of the unperceived object, which is a belief in its continued existence. This supposition of continued existence gets a force from memory and the tendency to regard perceptions of the same.

To justify his system, Hume explains four things. First, the problem arose because of the non-identity of interrupted perceptions, so he needs to say what the 'principle of identity' is. The principle of identity is unvaried 'uninterruptedness', since identity is temporal endurance or the idea of time or duration (THN 1.4.2.30; SBN 201). Time implies the succession of an unchangeable object. There is no such unchangeable object, so the imagination creates a fiction of an unchangeable object in order to make the passage smoother. Thus, the principle of a continuous identity is a fiction created in the imagination.

The second thing is to explain why the resemblances in interrupted perceptions impel us to attribute identity to them (THN 1.4.2.32; SBN 202). We are on the side of the vulgar here: there is no double existence involved, but 'only a single existence, which I shall call indifferently *object* or *perception*, according as it shall seem best to suit my purpose' (THN 1.4.2.31; SBN 202). Hume thinks the vulgar are correct in believing that there is only one kind of existence, and whether we call it an object, such as a hat or a door or whatever we call a collection of certain impressions is not important. Resemblance eases the transition in the imagination, allowing it to fill the missing parts of the fragmentary series from our memory of the previous continuous ones and in so filling them in we are postulating the existence of particulars which we have not on this occasion sensed, though we have sensed particulars of that like kind in the past. Hume adopts the 'general rule, that whatever ideas place the mind in the same disposition or in similar ones, are very apt to be confounded' (THN 1.4.2.32; SBN 203). When there is an uninterrupted perception, moments pass from one to another without any new perception being generated. Can some other objects put us in the same disposition? If so, then by the general rule, they are easily confused with identical objects. The answer is easy: 'related' objects can do the same thing, 'The thought slides along the succession with equal facility, as if it consider'd only one object; and therefore confounds the succession with the identity' (THN 1.4.2.34; SBN 204). This is what happens in perception. We have great constancy across interruption. The result is an easy transition which produces 'almost the same disposition of mind with that in which we consider one constant and uninterrupted perception. . .'Tis therefore very natural for us to mistake the one for the other' (THN 1.4.2.35; SBN 204).

The third aspect concerns the propensity to unite the broken perceptions. It is a certain principle that whenever there is conflict in the mind (as evidenced with the passions), there is uneasiness (THN 1.4.2.37; SBN 205). The converse strikes as well, 'whatever strikes in with the natural propensities, and either externally forwards their satisfaction, or internally concurs with their movements, is sure to give a sensible pleasure' (THN 1.4.2.37; SBN 205–6). There is uneasiness in the present conflict between identity and interruptedness. Which one is to give way? The 'smooth passage of our thought' moves us toward identification, so we give up the interruptedness. Yet, this does not seem satisfactory, in that with long intervals the perceptions are obviously interrupted. So it appears contradictory that they continue to exist without a mind. Hume argues that the interruption in the appearance of a perception does not necessary imply an interruption in its existence (THN 1.4.2.38; SBN 206). First, he needs to show how a perception can be absent from the mind without ceasing to exist. Hume's response is that the mind is a bundle of perceptions and any one perception may be broken off from it without ceasing to exist. Second, he needs to show an idea can become present to the mind without being a new existence. The broken-off idea can be returned to the bundle at a later time. Hume explains, 'The same continu'd and uninterrupted Being may, therefore, be sometimes present to the mind, and sometimes absent from it, without any real or essential change in the Being itself. An interrupted appearance to the senses implies not necessarily an interruption in the existence' (THN 1.4.2.40; SBN 207). This just establishes the possibility of the continued existence of perceptions, the lack of a contradiction. Since the mind has no access to this, it feigns continued existence; the imagination avoiding perplexity by the fiction of a continued existence.

Fourth, Hume explains the force and vivacity of the resulting idea. The supposition of continued existence amounts to belief. We believe the fiction because vivacity has been communicated to the idea by the lively ideas of memory. This is explained by the smoothness of the transition, wherein the vivacity of the original impression is retained 'without any great diminution' (THN 1.4.2.41; SBN 208). The same holds for vivid ideas of memory. Finally, we extend this beyond sensation and memory because 'objects, which are perfectly new to us, and of whose constancy and coherence we have no experience' resemble the constant and coherent perceptions (THN 1.4.2.42; SBN 209).

The exposition of the system has been completed. The belief in continued existence does not arise from the senses or reason, but only from the imagination, which is 'seduc'd into such an opinion' based on resemblance and the propensity of the imagination (THN

1.4.2.43; SBN 209). There are two fictions, that of identity and that of continued existence.

Now we turn back to independent existence and account for the 'many very curious opinions' that come with it (THN 1.4.2.44; SBN 210). First, experiments show that perceptions do not exist independently of the mind. Consider the simple experiment in which we press one eye with one finger and immediately perceive everything as double should convince us that all of our perceptions are dependent on our sense organs (THN 1.4.2.45; SBN 210). This has led philosophers to distinguish between perceptions and objects. The latter are uninterrupted and continue to exist. Now the vulgar are wrong in believing that what they see is continuous and distinct, and while the philosophers are correct in noting that all perceptions are dependent on, not distinct from, the mind, the philosophers are wrong in postulating two kinds of entities, perceptions and objects, and they are wrong in inferring objects from perceptions by causal reasoning. Hume argues that the philosophical system has no 'primary recommendation' either to imagination or reason (THN 1.4.2.47; SBN 211).

First, if we were to reason to the conclusion that objects exist independently of perceptions, then it could have to be causally. The only kind of reasoning which allows us to infer the existence of one thing from the existence of another thing is cause and effect. The inference is justified by experience. But our experience is only about the relations between and among perceptions because we only experience perceptions. We have no experience of the conjunction of perceptions and objects. So, we cannot reason our way to the existence of independent objects. How could the imagination make a transition to objects independent of perception? Hume challenges the reader for an answer, recognizing it is hard to prove a negative (THN 1.4.2.48; SBN 212). The supposition of a mind-independent object is not the proper subject for the imagination to work upon because we cannot imagine an object which is anything but a collection of perceptions.

The vulgar view and the view of the philosophers are contrary but connected. The philosophical system derived all its influence or authority from the vulgar system. This is a consequence of the claim that the philosophers' view has no 'primary recommendation' to reason or the imagination (THN 1.4.2.49; SBN 213). In effect, Hume is claiming that we would not have arrived at the philosophical system without having had problems with the vulgar system. It would have been an idle hypothesis if it did not solve some problem. Why should we not simply reject continued existence, except for the influence of the imagination which feigns it? The opinion that perceptions exist independently and continuedly and the opinion that they do not are in conflict. Which system lays claim to us varies with our circumstances: 'As long as our attention is bent upon the subject, the philosophical and study'd principle may prevail; but the moment we relax our thoughts, nature will display herself, and draw us back to our former opinion' (THN 1.4.2.51; SBN 214). Nature can even stop us in the middle of our thoughts. No strained metaphysical conviction of the dependence of perception will eradicate our natural belief that they exist independently and continuedly.

The philosophical system is supposed to get us out of this fix through the double existence hypothesis, which allows for the interruptedness and dependence of perception and the uninterruptedness and independence of objects. Hume calls this hypothesis a 'monstrous offspring of two principles, which are contrary to each other, which are both embrac'd by the mind' (THN 1.4.2.52; SBN 215). We cannot reconcile the two opinions, so 'we set ourselves at ease' by granting to each whatever it demands (THN 1.4.2.52; SBN 215). If we were fully convinced of either side, we would have no need for the compromise. Another advantage of the philosophical system is that it resembles the vulgar system in that it is easy to slip from one to the other. Philosophers do not 'neglect' this advantage and we find them 'immediately upon leaving their closets, [mingling] with the rest of mankind in those exploded opinions, that our perceptions are our only objects, and continue identically and uninterruptedly the same in all their interrupted appearances' (THN 1.4.2.53; SBN 216).

Two aspects of the system depend on the imagination. External objects are supposed to resemble the internal perceptions. This cannot be the result of causal reasoning. It is based on the hypothesis that all ideas in the imagination are borrowed from some preceding perception, and that 'We never can conceive any thing but perceptions, and therefore must make every thing resemble them' (THN 1.4.2.54; SBN 216). This applies to particular cases. We take a perception to resemble the particular object which caused it. We add resemblance to cause and effect to 'complete every union', which we have a strong propensity to do in every case (THN 1.4.2.55; SBN 217).

This ends the account of the systems with respect to the external world. At this point, Hume feels a 'contrary sentiment' and is no longer inclined to put favor in the evidence of the senses or the imagination, how can such trivial qualities of the fancy lead to 'solid and rational' system? (THN 1.4.2.56; SBN 217) The qualities have no perceivable connection to independent and continued existence. The vulgar system is just inconsistent and all the philosophical system does is invent a 'new set of perceptions' (THN 1.4.2.56; SBN 218). This is because we can only conceive particular ideas, 'to be in their nature any thing but exactly the same with perceptions' (THN 1.4.2.56; SBN 218). How can we place any confidence in this? This doubt arises whenever we consider the matter. This scepticism recurs and can never be totally eliminated. The only way to avoid it is by being careless and inattentive, that is, simply by ignoring the difficulties. Nature restores our beliefs, which after all are too important for her to trust to mere philosophical theorizing (THN 1.4.2.57; SBN 218). Whatever the case, the reader, as will himself, will continue to believe in both an internal and external world, despite what they think of the arguments.

8.3. ANCIENT PHILOSOPHY

Hume shows that two concepts of ancient philosophy correspond to fictions. The ancients used to talk of substance and substantial form, as the unchanging objects, and the sensible qualities such as color were thought to be accidents which inhered or resided in substance. The ancients attempt to explain the identity of objects despite change and the relationship between a thing and its parts both rely on substance but we have no idea of what a substance is and so they fail. These concepts are unintelligible, but they were invented in the same way that we invent fictions of continued and distinct existence. In the case of substance, Hume explains that the imagination 'is apt to feign something unknown and invisible, which it supposes to continue the same under all these variation and this unintelligible something it calls a *substance*' (THN 1.4.3.5; SBN 220).[9] Further, the imagination by 'the same habit, which makes us infer a connexion betwixt cause and effect, makes us here infer a dependence of every quality on the unknown substance' (THN 1.4.3.7; SBN 222).

There are three stages of opinion about the connections among objects or perceptions as people acquire 'new degrees of reason and knowledge' (THN 1.4.3.9; SBN 222). First, there is the vulgar view that there is an actual connection of objects. Second, there are the philosophers who see the folly of the vulgar view and seek to remedy it by the search for power or agency. But there is no power or agency, and the most that the false philosophers can hope for is the illusion of explanation provided by profound sounding but empty concepts such as a special faculty of the mind or an occult quality in objects (THN 1.4.3.10; SBN 224). The third stage of opinion is the true philosophy which accepts the vulgar view but recognizes that any connection among perceptions is supplied by the imagination through habit or custom.

8.4. MODERN PHILOSOPHY

The ultimate judge of all systems of philosophy is the imagination. The imagination has two sets of principles. The first set of principles is 'permanent, irresistible, and universal' and includes the association of ideas such as the inference from cause to effect (THN 1.4.4.1; SBN 225). This principle is the foundation of all thought and action and human nature would perish without it. Articulate voices in the dark are thought to be other persons. The second set of principles is 'changeable, weak and irregular' and is not necessary for either thought or action (THN 1.4.4.1; SBN 225). Some people when they hear articulate voices in the dark apprehend specters instead. The principles of the ancient philosophers are like specters in the dark. Ancient philosophy appeals to principles of the imagination that are 'changeable, weak and irregular', while the modern philosophy professes to appeal to the more 'permanent, irresistible, and universal' principles of the imagination (THN 1.4.4.2; SBN 226). Hume wonders whether the principles of the modern philosophy are of the right type, or whether instead they share the problems of the principles of the ancients. He finds the modern philosophy lacking, arguing that the fundamental principle of the modern philosophy, that ideas of primary qualities resemble their objects, while ideas of secondary qualities do not resemble anything in the object, is mistaken (see Chapter 2.3.3).

The fundamental principle of modern philosophy is the assertion that colors, sounds, heat and cold, that is the secondary qualities, are impressions in the mind and do not resemble anything like the qualities in the object. The chief argument is that from relativity, which

Hume illustrates by examples. Depending on our health, a sick person may be unable to eat food which usually pleases them very much; depending on the 'different complexions and constitutions of men', that which is bitter to one person is sweet to another', fire communicates pleasure at one distance and pain at another (THN 1.4.4.3; SBN 226).[10] The external object remains the same while the impressions vary depending on the circumstances. The conclusion drawn from this is that the same object cannot 'at the same time, be endow'd with different qualities of the same sense, and as the same quality cannot resemble impressions entirely different; it. . .follows, that many of our impressions have no external model' (THN 1.4.4.4; SBN 226). The key claim is that like effects have like causes. Since some impressions do not resemble their originals and since there is no difference among these and other impressions, none do, 'We conclude, therefore, that they are, all of them, derived from a like origin', so the secondary qualities are nothing but impressions in the mind that do not resemble anything in the object (THN 1.4.4.4; SBN 227).

It seems that the principle of primary qualities alone being real follows without difficulty, but Hume has a major problem with this move. The problem is that we cannot explain the primary qualities without reference to secondary qualities. Secondary qualities depend on the observer, therefore primary qualities are dependent upon the observer and cannot give us an idea of objects as distinct from perceptions. If qualities like colors have no mind-independent existence, then neither do the so-called primary qualities. For example, in order to explain motion, we must explain extension and solidity. It is impossible to conceive of extension without conceiving of 'simple and indivisible' parts which are colored and solid (THN 1.4.4.8; SBN 228). But what is it, Hume asks, that vision presents to the mind as extended? All we find is an array of colors. Color is not supposed to resemble the object, so the argument depends on solidity. But to have an idea of solidity, we must have an idea of objects which do not penetrate each other despite the utmost force. But how is this composed? Not of colors. Extension depends on solidity, as we have seen, so the idea of solidity requires circular reasoning (THN 1.4.4.9; SBN 229). The idea of solidity cannot depend on either the idea of motion or the idea of extension.

Another problem is the impression from which the idea of solidity is supposed to be derived. It is supposed to come from feeling, but this answer is 'more popular than philosophical' (THN 1.4.4.12; SBN 230). The feeling is different from the solidity. First, someone who has 'palsey in one hand' who cannot feel the table can see his hand to be supported by it. Second, impressions of touch are simple (THN 1.4.4.14; SBN 230). Yet, to replicate the situation where two stones resist each other, we would have to remove part of the impression, which is impossible for simple impressions. Third, solidity is invariable, while the feeling of resistance is variable. Solidity depends on the sense of touch. Since the sense of touch is just as variable as the other secondary qualities, we must conclude that solidity cannot resemble the object.

The upshot is that there is an opposition between reason and the senses. The former excludes colors, and so on, which then gets rid of the very object that the senses indicate have a continued and independent existence. In short, there is no way of inferring the existence of an object from any kind of quality.

8.5. THE IMMATERIAL SOUL

Having examined the question of the nature and existence of the external world, Hume now turns to nature and existence of the soul, the inner world. He expects to find the same difficulties with this area (THN 1.4.5.1; SBN 232). His main conclusion is that the notion of an immaterial soul is meaningless, and given his account of causal reasoning, matter may indeed be the cause of thought. However, this has no effect on religion.

Just as it seemed necessary to some philosophers to hypothesize the existence of a material substance for the support of our perceptions of the external world, it likewise seemed necessary to other philosophers to hypothesize the existence of an immaterial soul or mind in which the perceptions inhere. Descartes, for instance, asserted that the soul is an immaterial substance in which our perceptions inhere.

Hume wonders what is meant by the terms 'substance' and 'inherence'. If you have an idea of substance, then you must have an impression of substance. Following the Copy Principle, he challenges these philosophers to produce the impression of substance. Which among our many impressions is the one that represents the self? Does it come from sensation or reflection? Is it pleasant or painful? Does it endure, or does it come and go? Hume was confident that no

SCEPTICISM

answer could be given to these questions. In order to evade this challenge, philosophers may define substance as 'something which may exist by itself' (THN 1.4.5.5; SBN 233). As we observed at Chapter 4.3.2. Descartes and Spinoza both defined substance in this manner. The problem here is that everything satisfies this definition. To explain, Hume relies on the Separability Principle, that whatever is distinguishable can be separated by the imagination. The imagination can clearly separate the perceptions. Moreover, whatever can be conceived separately can exist separately. Therefore, perceptions can exist separately, we can think of anything, call it a mode or an accident, existing separately. Consequently, all perceptions fit the above definition of substance, so that the addition of the word substance adds nothing to our understanding. We have no need for the concepts of substance, nor inherence, which is 'suppos'd to be requisite to support the existence of our perceptions. Nothing appears requisite to support the existence of a perception. We have, therefore, no idea of inhesion' (THN 1.4.5.6; SBN 234).

A second argument for the immateriality of the soul is that matter is extended or has dimensions, whereas thought is not extended. Therefore, thought and the soul or mind cannot be material if they are not extended. Hume does not think that this argument proves that the soul is immaterial but it raises the question of the local conjunction of the soul with matter. Before we can answer this question, we must raise the still more general question of what objects in general are capable of a local conjunction.

Hume answers the question of a local conjunction by asserting that 'an object may exist, and yet be nowhere' (THN 1.4.5.10; SBN 235). Only the perceptions of sight and feeling occupy a place, therefore, only the perceptions of sight and feeling are capable of local conjunction. If I say that I am in love or I smell roses, it is silly to ask me where the passion of love or the smell is. You cannot say these perceptions are in the mind, since it is exactly the nature of mind or soul which we are trying to explain. The perceptions of sight and feeling, such as color and tangibility, are capable of local conjunction with each other, but they cannot be locally conjoined to the other perceptions. For example, I can say that the red spot is next to the blue spot, but I cannot say that the smell is next to the blue spot. It is still possible for a perception that has no place, such as the smell of roses, to have other relations with extended perceptions. For example, it is possible for the smell of roses to be related causally and by contiguity in time with certain objects which look red and have a certain feeling (THN 1.4.5.12; SBN 237). In fact, to talk of a particular smell as being the smell of roses means only that one perception, namely, a flower of a certain color, shape, structure is prior to and constantly contiguous with a certain smell, namely the smell of roses. The relations of causation and contiguity in time between extended perceptions and unextended perceptions lead the imagination to give them a new relation, namely, conjunction in place. This new relation is feigned in order to strengthen the original connection; the only reason for this is that the imagination simply feels a satisfaction in creating this fiction (THN 1.4.5.12; SBN 238).

To further critique the doctrine of the immateriality of the soul, Hume takes information about Spinoza from Bayle's *Dictionary* (see Chapter 2.3.6). The following summary of Spinoza's substance monism is given: The universe is composed of only one substance in which both thought and matter inhere. Everything else, whether it be a perception of the internal or external world is a modification of that single substance. Theologians offer three criticisms of Spinoza (THN 1.4.5.22; SBN 243). First, since a mode is not a distinct or separate existence, it must be the same thing as substance. Therefore, the distinction is incomprehensible. Second, matter and substance are the same thing. If substance can exist by itself, so can matter. Third, how can the same substance be modified into incompatible forms such as a round and a square table? The same criticisms can made against the theologians who hold the view that humans possess a soul that is a simple, indivisible and immaterial substance. Is it any less unintelligible to suppose that the diverse and 'even contrarieties' of perceptions are all modifications of a simple, uncompounded and indivisible substance? (THN 1.4.5.27; SBN 245) Second, every perception can exist by itself. Third, how can the same substance be modified into impressions which are both round and square?

Hume thinks that the only thing of which we actually have an idea or can speak intelligibly about is perception. The question of the material and the immaterial nature of the soul is meaningless; and the question of the local conjunction of our perceptions and substance is equally meaningless. The intelligible and more important question concerns the cause of our perceptions. The only connection we see between cause and effect is constant conjunction. The cause of thought and perception is motion, the motion of the body (THN 1.4.5.30; SBN 248). Should someone then object that we must explain the union of soul and body, Hume would reply that by soul and body we can mean only certain perceptions. When some perceptions are constantly conjoined to others, we say that they are causes and effects. The entire question can be answered without considering the problem of substance, mental or spiritual, and without considering the problem of local conjunction. In any case, the latter two problems are really unintelligible. Hume leaves us with a dilemma. Either we accept his theory that causation depends on constant conjunction or assert that causation depends on perceiving a connection in the objects. The trouble is that we never perceive a real connection in objects. If we assert that God is the ultimate cause of our volition, then He is the ultimate cause of our bad actions as well as our good actions (THN 1.4.5.21; SBN 249). As we saw in Chapter 7.3 when discussing the religious implications of necessity, Hume thinks this is a mysterious area, beyond the bounds of human reason and better off left alone.

Hume finally asserts that his arguments about the soul are not dangerous to religion. If he has undermined the metaphysical arguments for the immateriality of the soul, then this only proves the other arguments for the immateriality of the soul are stronger and more convincing. These other arguments are the moral arguments and the argument based on the analogy with nature. Hume does not discuss those arguments at this point, although he does present his thoughts on the matter in the suppressed essay 'Of the Immortality of the Soul'.

8.6. PERSONAL IDENTITY

Another topic in the inner world is that of personal identity.[11] The problem of identity of persons was particularly pressing in the eighteenth century. Not only do we need some account of identity of this sort in order to evaluate doctrines of immortality, but also the topic is important for morality, particularly responsibility, and divine punishment. Locke famously declared personal identity to be a 'forensic' notion, implying responsibility for actions and is needed for courts of law and the Day of Judgment (ECHU 2.27.26). He thought that what it is to be the same person has to do with what it is to be the appropriate subject for such things as divine and legal punishment. So, if A is the same person as B, then B is responsible for the actions of A. In order to deal out the appropriate divine and legal punishment, we need a theory by which we pinpoint when one must be considered the same person.

Philosophers think that we have a strong sense of self and that each sensation, emotion etc. confirms that it exists and continues to exist. Hume thinks this is contrary to experience. Hume's usual starting point, an investigation into the impression from which the idea of the self is to be derived, creates a difficulty for the self is not an impression, but rather that which 'has' impressions, the self is a reference point for the impressions and ideas. To produce an impression of the self would be to invite contradiction, since it would have to remain the same all through our life, while there is no constant and invariable impression. The impression of our self is not of an enduring self but of a bundle of varying perceptions, so it appears impossible to have any such idea of the self (THN 1.4.6.2; SBN 251). Further, by the Separability Principle, all perceptions are distinct and so capable of existing on their own. So how do they belong to the self? All Hume can find are individual perceptions. If you annihilate the perceptions, you annihilate the self.

Anyone who does not have this impression of the self ('the rest of mankind') is a bundle of perceptions in perpetual flux and rapid succession. He points out that when you start introspecting on the contents of your mind, you notice a bunch of different thoughts and feelings and perceptions and such in a perpetual state of flux, 'The mind is a kind of theatre, where several perceptions successively make their appearance; pass, re-pass, glide away, and mingle in an infinite variety of postures and situations' (THN 1.4.6.4; SBN 252–3). There is no identity or simplicity here. So as far as we can tell, there is nothing to the self over and above a big, fleeting bundle of perceptions. This is sometimes called 'The Bundle Theory of the Self'.

Despite this lack of impression of self, we still have a propensity to ascribe a certain identity to the collection of perceptions we find. That is, we still believe that there is a personal self. Why do we ascribe identity to successive perceptions? Here we have to take the matter 'pretty deep' and look at the identity of animals and plants, since there is a great analogy there (THN 1.4.6.4; SBN 253). In order to account for this propensity, Hume distinguishes between two interpretations of personal identity. The second interpretation, personal identity as it regards the passions, is discussed in Book 2 of the *Treatise*. For the present purpose, in Book 1, Part 4 of the *Treatise*, Hume accounted for the first interpretation of personal identity by

the propensity of the imagination to create fictions: we feign the existence of a continued self in order to remove the interruption of our
perceptions (THN 1.4.6.6; SBN 254). Although identity applies only
to what is invariable and uninterrupted, when there is enough similarity among perceptions to yield a smooth transition between distinct perceptions, we create a fiction of identity, confusing identity
with the notion of related objects. We disguise the absurdity behind
such notions as soul or substance, which is added to give us a
stronger or more unified concept of the self. We invent a fiction,
either of something invariable and uninterrupted or of something
mysterious and inexplicable 'connecting the parts beside their relation' (THN 1.4.6.6; SBN 255). We arrive at this idea in the same way
when we think of animals and plant as identical things persisting
over time. For example, a plant, an animal or a human being under-
goes vast or even complete change over a certain period of time, but
we still attribute an identity to the object.

This is all explained as usual by smooth transition of the imagination (THN 1.4.6.7; SBN 255). It can be seen by the fact that our
tendency to allow identity is relative to the size of the thing. A
change in a few inches would not affect the identity of a planet, but
it would that of a human body. Further, we are likely to allow identity where there is a common end or purpose of parts, and more so
when there is a sympathy between them (THN 1.4.6.11–2; SBN 257).
This is why we ascribe identity of plants and animals. This carries
over to personal identity, '[t]he identity, which we ascribe to the mind
of man, is only a fictitious one, and of a like kind with that which we
ascribe to vegetables and animal bodies' (THN 1.4.6.15; SBN 259).

The relations among perceptions that cause us to ascribe identity
to the human mind cannot be real connections discovered by the
understanding and must therefore be relations that lead us to associate these perceptions in the imagination. These relations are resemblance and causation. These relations produce a smooth transition in
our thought and lead us to create the fiction of personal identity, a
single continuous self extended through time (THN 1.4.6.17; SBN
260). When the change in perceptions is a small proportion or gradual
or seems to follow a common end, then memory produces the relation
of resemblance for ourselves and even for the identity we attribute to
others. Cause and effect is implicated in the regularity of perceptions.
The 'true' idea of the human mind consists of a system of different
perceptions 'link'd together by the relation of cause and effect, and

mutually produce, destroy, influence, and modify each other' (THN 1.4.6.19; SBN 261). Moreover, our knowledge of past pleasures and pains causes us to take a concern in our future pleasures and pains and this relation of causation aids us in producing the idea of identity. Hume compares the soul to a commonwealth, which retains its identity not by virtue of some enduring core substance, but by being composed of many different, related, and yet constantly changing elements, 'Whatever changes he endures, his several parts are still connected by the relation of causation' (THN 1.4.6.19; SBN 261).

Memory is also responsible for the relation of causation, since it is our memory of the past which influences our present and future concern. Memory is thus a 'source' of personal identity (THN 1.4.6.20; SBN 261). Without it, there would be no notion of causation or any notion of the 'chain of causes and effects which constitute our self or person' (THN 1.4.6.20; SBN 262). Memory actually discovers personal identity rather than producing it, since it reveals the causal relations among our perceptions. Once the notion of causation has been acquired from memory, we then 'extend the same chain of causes, and consequently the identity of our persons beyond our memory, and can comprehend times, and circumstances, and actions, which we have entirely forgot, but suppose in general to have existed' (THN 1.4.6.20; SBN 262). I would be hard-pressed for instance to explain my exact thoughts and actions on December 22nd 2006, let alone August 1st 2003 or May 11th 1999 or October 30th 1985, yet I still suppose that the present self is the same person with the self at each particular time. For those who think that memory produces personal identity entirely, it will be necessary to explain why we can extend our identity beyond our memory (THN 1.4.6.20; SBN 262).

In the Appendix to the *Treatise*, Hume famously expresses dissatisfaction with his account of the self. There he says his views involve him 'in such a labyrinth, that, [he] must confess, [he] neither [knows] how to correct [his] former opinions, nor how to render them consistent' (THN App. 10; SBN 633). After repeating the arguments, he says that the two principles he cannot render consistent are that:

(1) All our distinct perceptions are distinct existences and;
(2) That the mind never perceives any real connection among distinct existences.

There would be no difficulty if either our perceptions did either inhere in something 'simple and individual', or if the mind perceived 'some real connexion among them' (THN App. 21; SBN 636). Pleading 'the privilege of a sceptic', Hume confesses that this difficulty is 'too hard for [his] understanding' (THN App. 21; SBN 636). He hopes that someone in the future can remedy the difficulty.

No scholarly consensus has been reached as to exactly what the intended contradiction with the two principles is supposed to be, although a variety of accounts abound.[12] Some have even argued that the two principles are consistent and that the acceptance of (1) provides an explanation for (2). The two claims taken together then are not incompatible with each other but constitute the fundamental grounds for thinking that personal identity arises from associative principles of the imagination rather than from real connections among distinct existences.

In any case, it is worth emphasizing that in addition to his doubts, Hume expresses continued satisfaction with his theory of personal identity in the Appendix. He says his 'extraordinary' conclusion that we only feel a connection between the distinct perceptions and that our notion of personal identity arises from our psychological nature – our being creatures of custom and habit, 'need not surprise us' (THN App. 20; SBN 635–6). The doctrine illuminates what most philosophers are inclined to think, that personal identity arises out of consciousness and that consciousness 'is nothing but a reflected thought or perception' and further, that his theory has so far a 'promising aspect' (THN App. 20; SBN 635–6). Hume's shift from a moment of extreme despair to qualified satisfaction about his account of personal identity in the Appendix is indicative of the sort of sceptical attitude taken toward his own philosophy. As we shall see in the next two sections, Hume thinks in the end not only that we ought to adopt a sceptical attitude to our own philosophical judgments, but also that we ought to be as diffident about our doubts as about our beliefs.

8.7. EFFECTS OF SCEPTICISM ON PHILOSOPHY

So far, Hume has examined an argument to do with reason deemed very sceptical because the conclusion is that if left to the devices of reason alone, our confidence in any probability judgment would decrease to nothing if we consistently check our reasoning. He has also dealt with the opinions of the different schools of philosophy on four problems:

(1) The continued and distinct existence of objects
(2) The cause of our perceptions and
(3) The immaterial soul
(4) Personal identity

The first two problems concern philosophical systems of the external world and there are 'contradictions and difficulties in every system' (THN 1.4.5.1; SBN 232). The second two problems regard the philosophical systems of the internal world and here we must be content to leave much to the unknown. Other philosophers have attempted to solve the first two problems by distinguishing between perceptions and objects. Hume solves the problem by pointing out that the imagination creates the fiction of continued and distinct existence for the sake of convenience. Other philosophers attempted to solve the second two problems by appealing to an immaterial soul or a simple and identical self. Hume solves the problem by pointing to the constant conjunction of perceptions and by once more pointing out how the imagination creates the fiction of an identical self for the sake of convenience.

In the 'Conclusion of this Book', Hume surveys his results and sceptical despair strikes. The poor condition of our faculties has left him with feelings of solitude. He wonders why he can continue to do philosophy given that 'After the most accurate and exact of my reasonings, I can give no reason why shou'd assent to it; and feel nothing but a strong propensity to consider objects strongly in that view under which they appear to me' (THN 1.4.7.3; SBN 265). His view emphasizes experience that instructs us of past conjunctions of objects and habit, which leads to expectation regarding the interrelation of the past and future. Why should we believe what the memory tells us about the past or what habit predicts for the future? The answer lies in the capacity of the imagination to communicate vivacity from a present impression to the ideas of the past and the future. It is the imagination, which experience and habit operate upon together to produce intense and lively ideas.

There is also the disappointing and discouraging discovery that the necessity and power of causes is located in the determination of the mind and not in the object. Now this 'deficiency in our ideas is

SCEPTICISM

not, indeed, perceiv'd in common life' but that 'this proceeds merely from an illusion of the imagination; and the question is, how far we ought to yield to these illusions' (THN 1.4.7.6; SBN 267). This question leads to a dilemma. For if we don't want to follow every 'trivial suggestion of the fancy', we must adhere to reason, but from *Treatise* 1.4.1 we know that the understanding, when acting alone, 'entirely subverts itself, and leaves not the lowest degree of evidence in any proposition, either in philosophy or common life' (THN 1.4.7.7; SBN 267). We are left therefore with a choice between 'false reason and none at all' and that he knows 'not what ought to be done in the present case' (THN 1.4.7.7; SBN 268).

What happens next is surely one of the greatest expressions of sceptical doubt in the history of philosophy. Hume is reduced to a state of sceptical anguish, ready to abandon all belief and reasoning. He says that 'The *intense* view of these manifold contradictions and imperfections in human reason has so wrought upon [him], and heated [his] brain', that he is 'ready to reject all belief and reasoning, and can look upon no opinion even as more probable or likely than another' (THN 1.4.7.8; SBN 268–9). He then goes on to ask some serious questions to do with common life, questions to do with his origin, his future, how he should treat people, and so on: 'Where am I, or what? From what causes do I derive my existence, and to what condition shall I return? Whose favour shall I court, and whose anger must I dread? What beings surround me?' (THN 1.4.7.8; SBN 269) He is 'confounded' by all these questions, and 'in the most deplorable condition imaginable. . .and utterly depriv'd of the use of every member and faculty' (THN 1.4.7.8; SBN 269). Nature swoops in to rescue Hume from sceptical despair, forcing aside philosophical speculations and forcing a return to the normal activities of common life, indulging in his need for relaxation and entertainment. He recognizes, though, that in time he will be drawn back into philosophical speculation because of natural intellectual curiosity, that passion for truth, and to attack superstition and educate the world.

There can be no doubt that these sceptical arguments have a profound effect on belief and that we can and do keep such sceptical reflections before our minds when thinking in the study and about common life. The *Dialogues Concerning Natural Religion* is illuminating on this point. Reminiscent of the discussion of Descartes' antecedent scepticism at beginning of *Enquiry* Section 12, Philo

163

recommends scepticism about human faculties. He insists that we should 'Let the errors and deceits of our very senses be set before us', not to mention the insurmountable 'difficulties which attend first principles in all systems', and 'become thoroughly sensible of the weakness, blindness, and narrow limits of human reason', considering 'its uncertainty. . .even in subjects of common life and practice' (DNR 4). Philo's overall point is that, even when working with materials of 'common life and experience', human reason is feeble and defective, so when confronting such grand subjects as 'the origin of worlds', there is even less reason to trust 'this frail faculty' (DNR 4). Cleanthes responds that this sort of scepticism cannot be maintained in the face of everyday life. He jokes that the sincerity of Philo's scepticism will be learned as soon as the company breaks up: 'we shall then see whether you go out at the door or the window, and whether you really doubt if your body has gravity or can be injured by its fall, according to popular opinion derived from our fallacious senses' (DNR 5). On a more serious note, Cleanthes argues that although the sceptic may 'entirely renounce all belief and opinion' after 'intense reflection on the contradictions and imperfections of human reason', 'it is impossible for him to persevere in this total scepticism' in daily life (DNR 5).

Philo agrees, granting that sceptics must act, live, and converse like all others for no other reason than 'the absolute necessity' of doing so (DNR 6–7), but still points to the usefulness of scepticism. Acquiring the habit of 'sceptical considerations on the uncertainty and narrow limits of reason' carries over into 'reflection on other subjects', and that this affects at least one's 'philosophical principles and reasoning', if not also one's 'common conduct' (DNR 6). Total or absolute scepticism may be impossible as we are active beings, but Philo suggests that a good dose of scepticism can be persistent, and effective, both in the study and common life.

In the end, Hume recommends mitigated scepticism (EHU Sect. 12.3). There are two types of mitigated scepticism. The first type is durable and useful to cure the dogmatism, something humans are prone to. Mitigated scepticism deflates the pretensions of the arrogant intellectuals, revealing the emptiness of their metaphysical inquiries. To understand opposing arguments and entertain objections is important and the lessons of philosophy should make you conduct your opinions with more modesty and reserve. In general, a degree of doubt, caution and modesty should always accompany a just reasoner. Accurate and just reasoning are the only solution to the errors of abstruse philosophy, metaphysical jargon and popular superstitions. According to the second type, we should limit ourselves to the narrow capacities of human understanding and to such subjects that fall under daily practice and experience. Philosophy should stick to methodical description of common life. Avoiding all distant and high enquiries, it instead focuses on common life; the consideration of which our mental capacities have adapted, philosophical decisions being nothing but reflections on common life corrected and methodized.

8.8. SCEPTICISM AND THE SCIENCE OF HUMAN NATURE

The goal was to produce a scientific account of the operations of the human mind and the result is a system with just one kind of object, perception, and a few ways in which these are produced. Sensation provides us with the original perceptions, and all else is, at bottom, the workings of the imagination. Hume follows the same procedure throughout in *Treatise* 1.4. First, other arguments are disposed of with the demand that all ideas be referred to their impressions. Next, he shows that the imagination can only conceive of perceptions. Finally, he shows in what ways these perceptions are related by the imagination. For Hume, there is no problem of the existence of an external world, no problem with the self or how the mind and body are related. The only problem he faces concerns the relations between perceptions. Perceptions are the only things that exist in Hume's universe.

The imagination is at the core of our beliefs. Unless the imagination communicated vivacity, we could never reason beyond our present sense perceptions, we would never believe any argument about the past or the future: 'The memory, senses, and understanding are, therefore, all of them founded on the imagination, or the vivacity of our ideas' (THN 1.4.7.3; SBN 264). All of our reasoning from cause and effect depends on the communication of vivacity. Without the communication of vivacity from the present impression to the inferred idea, no inference would be believed. If the understanding attempts to operate without the communication of vivacity supplied by the imagination, then the result is total scepticism. Only when reason is mixed with the propensity supplied by the imagination can we believe and consequently act upon our beliefs.

He recognizes his philosophy is 'very sceptical' as it tends 'to give us a notion of the imperfections and narrow limits of human understanding' (AB 27; SBN 657). His philosophy is sceptical because he has shown that reason and the understanding are much more limited than we might first have thought.[13] They cannot explain by themselves how we form and retain beliefs about such things as causes and the continued and distinct existence of objects; that is, the work of the imagination and its propensities. The importance of scepticism for the project of the science of human nature is that it forces us to recognize that human reason has its limitations. Awareness of the limitations of human understanding means that one develops a proper modesty in light of the discoveries of the limitations and imperfections of our fallible faculties. If we do not heed to the limitations of reason, then we are apt to engage in bold and unfounded speculation such as we find in superstition and religion. Such speculation leads more often than not to disturbing influences upon the conduct of our life and action. Moreover, these bold speculations and unfounded hypotheses have prevented the development of a science of human nature.

Scepticism also fuels the passion for truth and falsehood in the moral sciences. To cure the state of sceptical despair when contemplating the results of his system, he dines, takes a walk, plays a game or has some fun with his friends. Once he has relaxed and collected himself, his mind naturally wanders once again to all those disputed subjects he has met during reading and conversation and the passion for truth rises again. He is 'uneasy to think [he] approve[s] of one object, and disapprove of another; call one thing beautiful and another deform'd; decide concerning truth and falsehood, reason and folly, without knowing upon what principles [he] proceeds' (THN 1.4.7.12; SBN 271). He finds himself drawn back to philosophy out of intellectual curiosity and ambition to educate humankind and to make a name for himself with his discoveries. Hume thinks in the end we ought to be as diffident about our doubts as about our beliefs, and mindful of the sceptical results, we continue to conduct our enquiry with due caution and modesty. This is the 'origin' of his philosophy (THN 1.4.7.12; SBN 271). Scepticism thus motivates as well as sets the limits of the science of human nature, and without it, no science of human nature would be possible.

Establishing a philosophical system on scepticism does not mean that all is uncertain, however. An advantage of staying within the boundaries of the science of human nature is that it allows for the attainment of truth and certainty. Hume says as much when considering those who might judge his philosophical system to be deeply sceptical: a science in which all is 'uncertain' (EHU 1.14; SBN 13). His response is to point out that:

> It cannot be doubted, that the mind is endowed with several powers and faculties, that these powers are distinct from each other, that what is really distinct to the immediate perception may be distinguished by reflection; and consequently, that there is a truth and falsehood, which lie not beyond the compass of human understanding (EHU 1.14; SBN 13–4).

The upshot is that if we stick within the confines of the science of human nature, then there is genuine truth and falsehood to be had and there is nothing uncertain about it. Due attention to the lessons of scepticism is necessary preparation for this investigation. An awareness of the imperfect state of our faculties and limitations of the human understanding sceptically seasons our minds so that we proceed with more caution and modesty not only in our enquiries, but also in daily life.

NOTES

1 Passmore (1952: 133); Flew (1986: 109).
2 Garrett (1996); Owen (1999); Stanistreet (2002). A classic discussion of Hume's scepticism comes from Fogelin (1985).
3 Owen (1994: 204).
4 This interpretation of Hume's sceptical argument is much indebted to Owen's 'Hume's Scepticism With Regard to Reason: *Treatise* 1.4.1' at the *Hume Symposium* presented at the Pacific Division Meeting of the American Philosophical Association, Portland, OR, March 24th 2006.
5 Bennett gives a nice explanation of Hume's point. The idea is not sinking probabilities but a widening margin of error: Set a probability at 'Prob(P) at $n \pm 0.1$; then at stage 2 I alter this to $n \pm 0.1 + k$; then at stage 3 to $n \pm 0.1 + k^*$ for some $k^* > k$; and so on. If this is carried on long enough, it would lead to a result whose margin of error is so wide as to make the probability assignment boring, or even vacuous', see Bennett (2001: 315).
6 I owe this way of putting the point to Fogelin's 'Hume's Scepticism' in Fate Norton (1993: 105).
7 'That is a point, which we must take for granted in all our reasonings' (THN 1.4.2.1; SBN 187).
8 See also Bayle's entry on Pyrrho (HD: 197f.).

9 Later he writes that the 'original substance. . .as the principle of union or cohesion among those qualities, and as what may give the compound object a title to be call'd one thing, notwithstanding its diversity and composition' (THN 1.4.3.5; SBN 221).

10 This example is in Locke's *Essay* (ECHU 2.8.16).

11 I am indebted in this section to Eric Steinberg for helpful clarifications about Hume's position on personal identity.

12 There has been much scholarly discussion on this issue; for a thorough canvassing of the secondary literature and a proposed account about Hume's doubts, see Garrett (1997: chapter 8).

13 This discussion of Hume's scepticism is partly inspired by Owen's 'Hume and the Irrelevance of Warrant', presented at *Hume Colloquium II*, Caraca, Brazil, June 2004, and also Garrett (1997: chapter 10).

BIBLIOGRAPHY

Allison, Henry E. (2004). *Kant's Transcendental Idealism: An Interpretation and Defense*, revised edition, New Haven: Yale University Press.

Anscombe, G. E. M. (1981). *The Collected Papers. II. Metaphysics and Philosophy of Mind*, Minneapolis: University of Minnesota Press.

Arnauld, Antoine, and Nicole, Pierre (1996). *Logic or The Art of Thinking*, Trans. J. V. Buroker, Cambridge: Cambridge University Press,

Ayers, Michael (1991). *Locke*, Vol. I, New York: Routledge.

Bacon, Francis (2000). *The New Organon*, Ed. Lisa Jardine and Michael Silverthorne, Cambridge: Cambridge University Press.

Baier, Annette (1991). *A Progress of Sentiments: Reflections on Hume's Treatise*, Cambridge, MA: Harvard University Press.

Basson, A. H. (1958). *David Hume*, Baltimore: Penguin Books.

Bayle, Pierre (1965). *Historical and Critical Dictionary: Selections*, Trans. R. Popkin, Indianapolis/Cambridge: Hackett University Press.

Beck, Lewis White (1978). *Essays on Kant and Hume*, New Haven: Yale University Press.

Bennett, Jonathan (1971). *Locke, Berkeley and Hume: Central Themes*, Oxford: Clarendon Press.

— (2001). *Learning from Six Philosophers*, Oxford: Oxford University Press Vol. 2.

Berkeley, George (1979). *Three Dialogues between Hylas and Philonous*, Ed. Robert Adams, Indianapolis: Hackett.

— (1982). *A Treatise Concerning the Principles of Knowledge*, Ed. Kenneth Winkler, Indianapolis: Hackett.

Broughton, Janet (1983). 'Hume's Scepticism about Causal Inferences', *Pacific Philosophical Quarterly*, 64: 3–18.

— (1987). 'Hume's Ideas about Necessary Connection', *Hume Studies* 13: 217–44.

Burton, John Hill (1846). *Life and Correspondence of David Hume*, Volume I, Edinburgh.

Capaldi, Nicholas (1975). *David Hume: The Newtonian Philosopher*, Boston: Twanye Publishing.

Chappell, V. C. (ed.) (1966). *Hume*, Garden City: Doubleday.

Costa, Michael (1989). 'Hume and Causal Realism', *Australasian Journal of Philosophy* 67: 172–90.

Coventry, Angela (2003). 'Locke, Hume, and the Idea of Causal Power', *Locke Studies* 3: 93–112.

— (2005). 'A Re-examination of Hume's Debt to Newton' in *Ensaios Sobre Hume (II Colóquio Hume)*, Universidade Federal de Minas Gerais, Belo Horizente.

— (2006). *Hume's Theory of Causation: A Quasi-Realist Interpretation*, Continuum Studies in British Philosophy, London: Continuum Books.

Craig, Edward (1968). 'Berkeley's Attack on Abstract Ideas', *Philosophical Review*, 425–37.

— (1987). *In the Mind of God and the Works of Man*, Oxford: Clarendon Press.

Dancy, J. (1987). *Berkeley: An Introduction*, Oxford: Blackwell.

Descartes, René (1985, 1993). *The Philosophical Writings of Descartes*, Trans. John Cottingham, Robert Stoothoff, and Dugald Murdoch, Vols. I and II, New York: Cambridge University Press.

Easton, P. (ed.) (1997). *Logic and the Workings of the Mind: The Logic of Ideas and Faculty Psychology in Early Modern Philosophy*, Vol. 5, Ridgeview Atascadero California.

Edwards, Paul (ed.) (1967). *The Encyclopedia of Philosophy*, Volume 2, New York: Macmillan.

Falkenstein, Lorne (1999). *Hume Studies*, Vol. XXV: 241–9.

Fate Norton, David (ed.) (1993). *The Cambridge Companion to Hume*, Cambridge: Cambridge University Press.

Fieser, James (ed.) (2000). *Early Responses to Hume's Metaphysical and Epistemological Writings. I. Eighteenth-Century Responses*, London: Thoemmes Press.

Flew, Antony (1961). *Hume's Philosophy of Belief: A Study of his First Enquiry*, New York: The Humanities Press.

— (1986). *David Hume: Philosopher of Moral Science*, Oxford: Basil Blackwell.

Fogelin, Robert (1985). *Hume's Skepticism*, London: Routledge.

— (2001). *Berkeley and the Principles of Human Knowledge*, London: Routledge.

Forbes, Graeme (1985). *The Metaphysics of Modality*, Oxford: Oxford University Press.

Frasca-Spada, Marina (1998). *Space and the Self in Hume's Treatise*, Cambridge, Cambridge University Press.

Galileo (1959). *Discoveries and Opinions of Galileo*, Trans. Stillman Drake, New York: Anchor Books.

Garrett, Don (1997). *Cognition and Commitment in Hume's Philosophy*, Oxford: Oxford University Press.

— (2003). 'The Literary Arts in Hume's Science of the Fancy', *Kriterion* 108: 161–179.

Greenberg, Leonard (1955). 'Necessity in Hume's Causal Theory', *The Review of Metaphysics* 8: 612–23.

Grieg, J. (ed.) (1932). *The Letters of David Hume*, Vols. I and II, Oxford: Clarendon Press.

Guyer, Paul (ed.) (1992). *The Cambridge Companion to Kant*, Cambridge: Cambridge University Press.

Hearn, Thomas (1970). 'General Rules in Hume's *Treatise*', *Journal for the History of Philosophy* 8: 405–22.

Hobbes, Thomas (1994). *Leviathan*, Ed. Edwin Curley, Indianapolis/ Cambridge: Hackett University Press.

Holden, Thomas (2002). 'Infinite Divisibility and Actual Parts', *Hume Studies* 28: 3–25.

Home, Henry (Lord Kames) (1758). *Essays on the Principles of Morality and Natural Religion* (second edn), London: C. Hitch, L. Hames and others.

Howson, Colin (2000). *Hume's Problem: Induction and the Justification of Belief*, Oxford: Oxford University Press.

Hume, David (1885). *The History of England from the Invasion of Julius Caesar to the Revolution in 1688*, 6 vols. New York: John B. Alden.

— (1975). *An Enquiry Concerning Human Understanding and Concerning the Principles of Morals* (third edn). Eds. L. A. Bigge and P. H. Nidditch, Oxford: Clarendon Press.

— (1978). *A Treatise of Human Nature* (second edn), Eds. P. H. Nidditch and L. A. Selby-Bigge, Oxford: Clarendon Press.

— (1985). *Essays: Moral, Political, and Literary* (revised edn), Ed. Eugene Miller, Indianapolis: Liberty Fund.

— (1998). *An Enquiry Concerning the Principles of Morals*, Ed. T. L. Beauchamp, Oxford: Oxford University Press.

— (1998). *Dialogues Concerning Natural Religion* (second edn.), Ed. Richard H. Popkin, Indianapolis/Cambridge: Hackett University Press.

— (1999). *An Enquiry Concerning Human Understanding and Concerning the Principles of Morals*, Ed. T. L. Beauchamp, Oxford: Oxford University Press.

— (2000). *A Treatise of Human Nature*, Eds. D. F. Norton and M. J. Norton, Oxford: Oxford University Press.

Hurlbutt, Robert H. (1963). *Hume, Newton, and the Design Argument*, revised edition, University of Nebraska Press.

Jacobson, Anne (1989). 'Inductive Scepticism and Experimental Reasoning in Moral Subjects in Hume's Philosophy', *Hume Studies* 15: 325–38.

Jones, Peter (1982). *Hume's Sentiments: Their Ciceronian and French Context*, Edinburgh: Edinburgh University Press.

Kant, Immanuel (1997). *Critique of Pure Reason*, Trans. P. Guyer, Cambridge: Cambridge University Press.

— (1997). *Prolegomena to Any Future Metaphysics That Can Qualify as a Science*, Trans. Paul Carus, Chicago: Open Court.

Kemp Smith, Norman (1941). *The Philosophy of David Hume: A Critical Study of its Origins and Central Doctrines*, London: Macmillan.

Laird, J. (1932). *Hume's Philosophy of Human Nature*, London: Methuen.

Laudan, Larry (1981). *Science and Hypothesis*, Reidel: Dordrecht.

Leibniz, G. W. (1989). *Philosophical Essays*, Trans. Roger Ariew and Daniel Garber, Indianapolis/Cambridge: Hackett University Press.

Livingston, David (1984). *Hume's Philosophy of Common Life*, Chicago: University of Chicago Press.

Locke, John (1975). *An Essay Concerning Human Understanding*, Ed. P. H. Nidditch, Oxford: Oxford University Press.

Losee, John (1992). 'Hume's Demarcation Project', *Hume Studies*: 51–62.

Mach, Ernst (1960). *The Science of Mechanics* (sixth edition), Trans. Thomas J. McCormack, La Salle: Open Court.

Mackie, John (1974). *The Cement of the Universe: A Study of Causation*, Oxford: Clarendon Press.

— (1976). *Problems from Locke*, Oxford: Clarendon Press.

Malebranche, Nicolas (1997). *The Search After Truth*, Eds. Thomas Lennon and Paul Olscamp, Cambridge: Cambridge University Press.

Matthews, Michael R. (ed.) (1989). *The Scientific Background to Modern Philosophy: Selected Readings*, Indianapolis/Cambridge: Hackett University Press.

Mossner, Ernest (1947). 'The Continental Reception of Hume's *Treatise*', *Mind* LVI: 31–43.

— (1980). *The Life of David Hume* (second edition), Oxford: Clarendon Press.

Newman, Rosemary (1981). 'Hume on Space and Geometry', *Hume Studies* VII (1): 1–31.

Newton, Isaac (1952). *Opticks*, Mineola: Dover.

— (1962). *The Mathematical Principles of Natural Philosophy*, 2 volumes, Trans. and ed. Andrew Motte, revised by Florian Cajori, Berkeley: University of California Press.

Noxon, J. (1973). *Hume's Philosophical Development*, Oxford: Oxford University Press.

Owen, David (1994). 'Reason, Reflection, and Reductios', *Hume Studies* XX (2).

— (1999). *Hume's Reason*, Oxford: Oxford University Press.

Passmore, John (1952). *Hume's Intentions*, Cambridge: Cambridge University Press.

Pears, D. (1990). *Hume's System: An Examination of the First Book of His Treatise*, Oxford: Oxford University Press.

— (ed.) (1963). *David Hume: A Symposium*, London: Macmillan.

Penelhum, Terence (1975). *Hume*, New York: St. Martin's Press.

Parkinson, G. H. R. (1988). *An Encyclopedia of Philosophy*, London: Routledge.

Phalen, A. K. (1977). 'Hume's Psychological Explanation of the Idea of Causality', *International Philosophical Quarterly* 17: 43–57.

Pitcher, G. (1977). *Berkeley*, The Arguments of the Philosophers, London: Routledge & Kegan Paul.

Prichard, H. A. (1950). *Knowledge and Perception*, Oxford: Clarendon Press.

Reid, Rupert, and Richman, Kenneth (eds.) (2000). *The New Hume Debate*, London: Routledge.

Reid, Thomas (2001). 'Of Power', *The Philosophical Quarterly* 51: 3–12.

Rollin, Bernard (1971). 'Hume's Blue Patch and the Mind's Creativity', *The Journal of the History of Ideas*, 32: 119–28.

Russell, Paul (1995). *Freedom and Moral Sentiment: Hume's Way of Naturalizing Responsibility*, Oxford: Oxford University Press.

Schmitt, F. (1995). *Truth: A Primer*, Boulder, CO: Westview Press.

Sosa, Ernest, and Tooley, Michael (eds.) (1993). *Causation*, Oxford: Oxford University Press.

Stanistreet, Paul (2002). *Hume's Scepticism and the Science of Human Nature*, Aldershot, Ashgate.

Stewart, M. A. (ed.) (1990). *Studies in the Philosophy of the Scottish Enlightenment*, Oxford: Oxford University Press.

Stove, D. C. (1973). *Probability and Hume's Inductive Skepticism*, Oxford: Clarendon Press.

Strawson, Galen (1987). 'Realism and Causation', *Philosophical Quarterly* 37: 253–77.

— (1989). *The Secret Connexion: Causation, Realism and David Hume*, Oxford: Clarendon Press.

Stroud, Barry (1977). *Hume*, London: Routledge & Kegan Paul.

Taylor, R. (1963). 'Causation', *The Monist* 47: 287–313.

Thomson, Garrett (2003). *Bacon to Kant: An Introduction to Modern Philosophy*, (second edition), Prospect Heights, Ill.: Waveland Press.

Walsh, W. H. (1972). 'Hume's Concept of Truth', in *Reason and Reality: Royal Institute of Philosophy Lectures*, Volume V, London: Macmillan.

Watkins, Eric (2004). 'Kant's Model of Causality: Causal Powers, Laws, and Kant's Reply to Hume', *Journal of the History of Philosophy* 42: 449–88.

Watson, Brandon (2003). 'The Humean Lot', available at http://ots.utoronto.ca.users/branemrys/HLNotes.html.

Waxman, Wayne (1994). *Hume's Theory of Consciousness*, Cambridge: Cambridge University Press.

Woolhouse, Roger (1988). *The Empiricists*, Oxford: Oxford University Press.

Wright, John (1983). *The Sceptical Realism of David Hume*, Manchester: Manchester University Press.

— (1991). 'Hume's Rejection of the Theory of Ideas', *History of Philosophy Quarterly* 8: 149–62.

INDEX

abstract or general ideas 22, 23,
   53–6
  and aesthetics 130–1
  and morals 130–1
  and necessary connections 109,
   131–2
  and space and time 62–3, 74
Addison, Joseph 26
aesthetics, theory of 71–2, 123–34
Allison, Henry 101
ancient philosophy 151–2
Anscombe, G.E.M. 104n. 11
Arnauld, Antoine 19, 21, 64
  on infinite divisibility 59
Aristotle 50, 63
association of ideas 22, 37, 47–56,
   85, 87, 90, 92–4, 95, 152,
   159–60
Ayers, Michael 27n. 17

Bacon, Francis 16, 17, 32
Baier, Annette 77n. 21, 98
Barfoot, Michael 27n. 12
Basson, A. H. 119
Bayle, Pierre 5, 17, 64, 156, 167n. 8
  on infinite divisibility 25, 59
  on space 24–5
Beck, Lewis White 103n. 3
belief 89–94, 141, 165
  causes of 92–4
  and the existence of external
   objects 146, 148–50
  influence of 94

Bennett, Jonathan 41, 44, 136n. 36,
   167n. 5
Berkeley, George 14, 17, 50, 51,
   54
  on abstraction 23–4
  on immaterialism 22
  on infinite divisibility 61
  on knowledge 16
  on primary and secondary
   qualities 23
Biro, John 36n. 3
blue, missing shade of 41–4
Boileau, Nicolas 26
Bolingbroke, Henry St John 26
Boswell, James 10–11
Boyle, Robert 26
Broughton, Janet 135n. 15
Butler, Joseph 6, 26, 32

Capaldi, Nicholas 36n. 2, 136n. 36
cause 18, 22, 47, 49, 78–103,
   105–34
Cicero 26, 124
Clarke, Samuel 26
  on the causal maxim 83
Copernicus, Nicolaus 14
copy principle 37, 38–46
  and abstract ideas 55
  and cause and effect 81
  and the immateriality of the soul
   154–5
  and necessary connection
   106–110

vacuum 18, 22, 63–7
Voltaire 8
von Pufendorf, Samuel 26

Walsh, W. H. 70
Warburton, William 8
Watkins, Eric 107n. 4

Waxman, Wayne 76n. 6, 104n. 13
will 112–13
Woolhouse, Roger 136n. 36
Wright, John 76n. 5, 76n. 20,
  115–17

Zeno of Elea 17, 24–5